PIXAR STORYTELLING

Rules for Effective Storytelling Based on Pixar's Greatest Films

SECOND EDITION

Pixar Storytelling
Rules for Effective Storytelling Based on Pixar's Greatest Films
SECOND EDITION

ASIN: 9781717736406

ABOUT THE AUTHOR

Dean Movshovitz graduated from Tel Aviv University's Film and Television department, majoring in Screenwriting. After his studies, he served as Director of Film and Media at Israel's Office for Cultural Affairs in North America, at the Consulate General of Israel in New York. He won his first screenwriting award in Israel at age sixteen, for a short comedy script. Dean wrote about cinema for *Taste of Cinema* and the *Tel Aviv Cinematheque* magazine and has lectured widely about Israeli cinema during his tenure at the consulate. He has moderated filmmaker Q & A panels at Lincoln Plaza Cinemas, Film Forum, Jacob Burns Film Center, and many more organizations. His previous collaboration with Bloop Animation has been covered by The A.V. Club, Daily Dot, and other sources.

CONTENTS

4   Drama and Conflict   35

5   Pixar's Structure   49

6   Casting Characters   65

7 Villains 73

8 Developing an Idea 81

9 Endings 87

INTRODUCTION

Pixar represents the rare case of a studio becoming a distinct cinematic voice, loved by audiences, critics, and filmmakers alike. One of the main reasons for its success is the storytelling choices it favors and promotes. As much as Pixar's films are known for their rich fictional worlds, glorious visuals, and original plots, it is their uncanny ability to move audiences deeply that astonishes us with every new film the studio releases, causing grownups to tear up right next to their children. Pixar chooses stories and develops them in extremely satisfying and deeply moving ways. Despite transporting us to vastly different worlds with each film, Pixar's storytelling approach remains consistent.

I will explore these consistent Pixar storytelling techniques in this book. A deep look into the studio's films reveals certain repeated patterns. Some are universal and obvious to any budding screenwriter, in which case Pixar's exemplary use of these techniques can serve as a beacon. Some of the more idiosyncratic patterns of storytelling may illuminate the secrets behind the studio's success. This book will examine and uncover the mechanisms and patterns that make Pixar's films work so well.

One note to take into consideration: This book focuses only on Pixar's storytelling techniques and will neglect myriad other storytelling options that have proven to be successful, evocative, and moving. Despite the many risks Pixar takes and its dedication to endowing each of its films with a rare amount of heart and integrity, the studio still makes big-budget, family-friendly films that appeal to the masses. These movies are the focus of this work. I firmly believe that each of the patterns discussed here will prove useful to any film project—whether it's short or feature length, live action or animated, aimed toward Hollywood, Sundance, or Cannes.

CHAPTER 1

CHOOSING AN IDEA

*"Everything that made that giant tree is already
contained inside this tiny little seed.
All it needs is some time, a little bit
of sunshine and rain, and voilà!"*
—Flik

Mother Lodes—Choosing Ideas That Have a LOT of Potential

Choosing an idea for your film is a bit like selecting where to set up a gold mine. Some places will offer you a few nuggets, and in others you'll hit the mother lode. Both starting points can be the basis for a great story—those nuggets are still gold—but "mother lodes," those relatable ideas that offer many levels of clear drama and narrative options, tend to be easier to develop and more accessible to audiences.

Clearly, Pixar goes for the mother lodes. Part of the studio's success comes from its ability to recognize and develop strong, engaging ideas, which usually come with powerful, built-in emotional weight. These ideas evoke a rich exotic world (whether monsters, toys, or superheroes) that offers many possibilities for imaginative set pieces, visual richness, and original scenes. More importantly, these ideas contain tremendous physical and emotional stakes, which makes them immediately enticing and accessible.

Leaving the Comfort Zone: More Discomfort = More Story

How do you shape a story idea to include emotional stakes? Most good stories revolve around watching a character struggle outside of his or her comfort zone. Pixar continually figures out what a protagonist wants most—and then throws the exact opposite at them. This state of discomfort is gold for writers for a couple of reasons.

On a narrative level, it simply creates scenes. It gives you, as a writer, immediate material with which to work. If you're writing about a rat trying to cook in a sewer, it might be cute and even original, but not necessarily interesting or dramatic. But if you're writing about a rat trying to cook in a gourmet restaurant, narrative questions immediately arise: How does he get in? How can he do it on a regular basis? What happens when someone sees him? What happens when his dishes turn out great? All these questions lead to story strands that can be explored and harvested. All it took was placing a character in the most challenging setting he could be in.

On a different, deeper level, your idea must force your characters to go through an emotional journey. A character, forced out of its element, is compelled to work hard to get back to its comfort zone, just as we would in life. This desire propels actions, decisions, and emotions, which are the meat of your story's inner narrative. *Toy Story*'s concept of "toys are actually alive" is an immediately exciting one that offers many narrative possibilities and a rich world to explore. However, it isn't until the concept evolves into "favorite toy gets replaced by a newer, shinier toy," that emotional stakes are introduced.

In *Toy Story*, Buzz Lightyear's arrival completely upends Woody's cherished and seemingly natural status as Andy's favorite toy. Woody's reactions to this event end up sending him on a wild adventure that leads him to extremely uncomfortable situations: lost by his owner and trapped in Sid's basement. Buzz's popularity is the worst thing that could have happened to Woody, who has always been complacent about his role as leader among Andy's toys. This event also forces Woody to face many hard emotional truths. He realizes Andy's love cannot be taken for granted and that he might someday grow tired of Woody. Woody's struggle to keep his friends as they shun him and the fear he experiences when Andy drives off without him and Buzz, both come from deep emotional distress. These fears receive a distorted physical manifestation in Sid's abused toys. At the end of the movie, while the toys are again nervous about Andy's birthday, Woody is calmer. He turns to Buzz and says, "What could be worse than you?" He feels stronger and more confident of his role in Andy's life after his ordeal with Buzz (though the arrival of a puppy does surprise them both).

This discomfort is more than just bad luck or a worst-case scenario. It is a catalyst that forces our hero to react, and in the best movies, to grow and change. Discomfort isn't always rooted in a negative development: Wall-E's peaceful routine is upended by Eve's arrival. While it's great that he's no longer alone, Wall-E must now devise ways of winning over Eve's heart, or risk missing this opportunity to fulfill his dreams, possibly the last chance he'll get. If he fails, he'll be worse off than he was before. Eve's arrival makes Wall-E's life more challenging, and certainly less comfortable than it was.

To truly upset a character, you must create a weakness or fear that you can tap into. Therefore, Pixar creates a pre-existing problem in each protagonist's world.

A Character and World That Vie for Adventure—The Existing Flaw

As most of us go about our lives—working, dating, socializing—we tend to ignore things that are bothering us. Maybe it's a relationship we don't quite understand, a loss we haven't properly mourned, or a part of ourselves we haven't quite accepted. These emotional cracks are what makes us human, and they are what will make your characters compelling.

Ideally, even before the gears of the plot start to turn, there should be a problem in your protagonist's life or world. In *Monsters Inc.*, Waternoose complains that there is an electricity shortage because children don't scare as easily as they did in the past. In *Finding Nemo*, Marlin dotes on his son, suffocating him and denying him any sense of independence. This *flaw* is nowhere sharper drawn than in *Wall-E*, where the entire planet is decrepit. Of course, the flaw can be subtler than these examples. It could be Carl's broken heart and sense of purposelessness in *Up*.

Once you have found the *existing flaw* in your core idea, craft a story that pushes it to the extreme. The overprotective Marlin loses his son. The heartbroken Carl is about to lose his last connection to his life with Ellie—the house. Whatever the existing flaw, it must be clearly related to the plot you have crafted for your protagonist. The more these two work in tandem, the higher the emotional stakes will be and the more invested your audience will be.

Economy: How Every Moment in *Ratatouille* Stems from Its Core Idea

Pixar's films find the heart of their stories and never stray from it. Once they find the emotional core—the flaw and the plot that infringes on it—they make sure every development and every character are closely connected to this main narrative undertow.

Let's take a closer look at *Ratatouille*. Even before we meet Remy, we are introduced to the exuberant chef Gusteau and snooty critic Anton Ego. They clash over Gusteau's statement that "Anyone can cook." This prologue may seem extraneous. It doesn't have any actual bearing on Remy's adventures, and the movie's events would be clear without it. Yet this prologue is a crucial part of *Ratatouille*, because it sets up the thematic core of the film and the movie's real antagonist, Anton Ego.

When we meet Remy, he is a torn individual. He is a rat but is averse to the rats' way of living: stealing, eating garbage indiscriminately, and living by strict rules in packs. He is drawn to what he considers human living—exploring one's creativity, enjoying exciting flavors, experiencing and expressing individuality and curiosity. Remy's desires are at extreme odds with who (and what) he is.

The screenwriters of the film go out of their way to show us why this is a problem. We see how Remy's curiosity gets him in trouble, whether he is struck by lightning trying to cook a mushroom or getting shot at by an old lady when he reads her cookbook and steals her food. His father is also a problem. He chastises Remy for his passion, mocks him and pressures him to stick to the rats' traditional ways. Every element discussed here pertains to Remy's predicament. The old woman is the first instance of rejection by the human world. His father symbolizes rejection from the rat world. Emile, his brother, is a friend, but a contrast against which Remy's peculiarities stand out. Gusteau is established as Remy's sole mentor and guide.

At the end of the first act, after Remy's food excursions get the rat colony discovered and force all of them to relocate, Remy loses the group. He finds himself using Gusteau's book as a lifeboat, standing in front of a fork in the road. Yes, this is the sewer system, and Remy must gamble on which path to choose to find his friends and family. On a deeper level, this prolonged moment represents Remy's decision about himself: Will he follow his human side or his rat side? Even this small, physical, throwaway moment is used again to tap into the core idea of the story—Remy's split identity. It is no coincidence that Remy's choice leads him to Gusteau's restaurant in Paris.

These elements will continue to appear throughout the film as often as possible. Some in major ways, such as the sequence when Remy first enters the kitchen to fix the soup, yet must avoid being seen, burned, stepped on, or cooked. It is a perfect, dialogue-less presentation of the dangers he faces, and it's delivered as an action scene. Even Remy's casual wave to a human biker that causes the surprised man to crash is part of the core idea. On the other hand, when Remy starts allowing a growing group of rat friends to steal from Gusteau's, we see how Remy is still drawn to his rat community. Remy cannot reconcile the two sides of his personality.

The core question of *Ratatouille* is "Can this rat become a gourmet cook?" The first act shows all the reasons why he can and why he can't. Every scene that follows is an escalation of those reasons, with the answer swinging like a pendulum from "Yes, look at Remy and Linguini cooking together and becoming friends" to "No, no matter how talented he is, Remy will never be recognized as a cook on his own because he does not belong among humans, who will never accept him."

This is economy. Everything in your screenplay should relate to your core idea, to your main conflict. In *Ratatouille,* all the supporting characters reflect Remy's conflict. Consider Linguini. He is the negative image of Remy. He is the son of acclaimed chef Gusteau, but he can't cook and no one expects him to, because of his awkward demeanor. When he surprises them (with Remy's help), he gets a chance, thanks to Gusteau's credo. Colette serves as Gusteau's spokeswomen in the kitchen and as a mentor to Linguini. When they become close, Linguini dismisses Remy in favor of his romance with Colette—a powerful moment of human rejection that almost makes Remy give up on his dream.

Skinner is the opposite of Colette. He despises Linguini, partially because of his fear that Linguini will inherit the restaurant, but mostly because he refuses to believe that this silly boy can cook—a negative echo of the core idea. Skinner is also the first person to acknowledge Remy's existence and talents. He offers another, different, threat from the human world. He doesn't want to destroy Remy but instead to enslave him and use him to concoct a demeaning line of frozen food products using Gusteau's name. Even the rest of the cooks in the kitchen are fleshed out in a short monologue by Colette describing their various exciting backgrounds. She describes them as "pirates"—something Remy can relate to. This scene once again reinforces Gusteau's credo and the validity of Remy's dreams.

This brings us to two additional important characters in *Ratatouille*: Gusteau and Anton Ego, the angel and the devil of the film. It's almost as if these two dialectic paragons made a bet on whether anyone can cook and used Remy as a test case. Gusteau constantly whispers principles, encouragements, and guidance in Remy's ear, while Ego uses his power to put pressure on Skinner, Linguini and the cooks, threatening them with ridicule and embarrassment. These characters are also echoes of Remy's torn personality.

Gusteau believes in him and eggs him on in his journey. Ego, in turn, is the last and highest hurdle Remy must pass. If Remy can impress Ego enough with his cooking and be accepted as a cook, then his problems are over. The flaw he had at the beginning of the film will be resolved; he will find his place in the world and attain self-acceptance. Some of these ideas are stated outright in the film, and some are insinuated, such as in the film's prologue.

These elements are put in place to set up the film's final act, when Ego comes in to dine. Linguini finally shares his secret (Remy) with the cooks, who all leave him. Only Remy is left in the kitchen to cook during the dinner rush. When Remy's father sees Linguini coming to Remy's aid and understands the dangers Remy puts himself in to pursue his passion, he is moved. He puts the rat colony at Remy's disposal, leading to the potent visual of hundreds of rats running the kitchen during the dinner rush. This moment serves as a resolution to Remy's relationship with his father and the rat world; he is accepted by them. And clearly, it demonstrates that rats *can* cook. Colette returns, accepts the situation, and for the first time works together with Remy, thus resolving the tension in the Remy-Linguini-Colette triangle. The only open thread is Ego.

Remy chooses the dish to serve him, the titular Ratatouille, and makes it with Colette. In one of the film's most memorable moments, the dish sends Ego back to his childhood, to an innocence he had before he developed his snooty ideals. He insists on talking to the chef. This time Linguini and Colette give Remy his dues and introduce him to Ego after the restaurant closes. In Ego's glowing review he writes:

> "In the past, I have made no secret of my disdain for Chef Gusteau's famous motto: Anyone can cook. But I realize, only now do I truly understand what he meant. Not everyone can become a great artist, but a great artist can come from anywhere."

That seals the deal. Gusteau has won the argument—anyone can cook. Once Ego is on board, and after his father's help and acceptance, Remy can now reconcile the two parts of his personality. This is clearly evidenced in the film's closing moments, when Remy regales this tale to his rat friends before being called into the kitchen by Colette to serve Ego, the owner of this new restaurant. Of course, the dish is Ego's favorite, Ratatouille.

Summary

Every moment in *Ratatouille* evolved out of its core idea. The same should be true for any story you write. Once you have a good idea, such as one of those discussed in the first part of this chapter, treat it as a seed that you must sprout into story. Let it grow, step by step, hewing close to its core. What isn't part of this essence, this seed, probably shouldn't be part of your story and should be pruned mercilessly.

Uncomfortable characters are so appealing because we all like feeling comfortable. And once our cushy existence is taken from us, we need to reconcile these new circumstances with who we are and what we have lost. This desire creates scenes and conflicts for your characters and story. Pixar's characters go to great lengths to retrieve what they have lost. Watching them react to their new circumstances, fighting, and growing, is what makes Pixar's films so moving and enjoyable. From an extremely nervous father, a small fish who crosses an enormous ocean to learn how to let his son live; to a superhero stuck in retirement in the most mundane of lives; to a reclusive, heartbroken old man who must take responsibility over an innocent child; to an aspiring monster that just isn't scary—Pixar excels in putting characters in the worst places possible for them.

In *Inside Out*

Clearly, *Inside Out* has a "mother lode" of an idea. Choosing to set the film inside a character's head immediately offers myriad options for unique characters and set pieces. It is a wildly original, very appealing idea. Who wouldn't want to see what makes them tick? The emotional stakes are also practically built in: This world is a person's mind and heart, and its collapse would mean the destruction of that person, in this case, an 11-year-old girl named Riley.

Discomfort attacks Joy, the film's protagonist, from two fronts. First, she is pushed outside of her familiar position in Headquarters into an uncharted world, where she is vulnerable. (She could be forgotten or turned into an abstract thought.) On an emotional level, she must also cooperate with Sadness, whom she has never accepted or understood. Discomfort is also thrown at Riley, the person in whose mind the film takes place. She moves with her parents to a different city and, without Joy in Headquarters, can't feel happiness. As a matter fact, the collapse of Riley's mindscape is an apt metaphor for what discomfort should do to your characters. Your story should threaten to destroy their Islands of Personality, and they must protect them or create new ones.

The existing flaw is hinted at very early on in *Inside Out*. Headquarters has a problem: They don't know the purpose of one of their core members, Sadness. Joy obsessively works to keep Riley constantly happy, ignoring and even removing

Sadness, even though Sadness has a role in Riley's psyche, as evidenced early in the film when Joy confides with us: "I'm not actually sure what she does." When audiences hear that line, somewhere in the back of their heads they know that by the end of the film, Sadness's purpose will be discovered and it will be meaningful.

Do It Yourself: *What is the core idea of your story? Does it offer many possibilities for dramatic moments? Does it impart strong, specific emotional discomfort to your protagonist? Do you mine this discomfort to create scenes and movements that affect your characters emotionally? What is the flaw in your fictional universe? Is it closely related to the plot you constructed? Do they mutually enhance and enrich each other? Do all your characters, narrative decisions, scenes, and themes pertain to your core idea? Are you constantly exploring and expanding the seed of your story as it progresses? Have you branched off in directions that aren't part of your core idea?*

CHAPTER 2

CREATING COMPELLING CHARACTERS

"You are a sad, strange little man."
—Buzz Lightyear

Interesting Characters Care Deeply

Once you have a strong idea for a movie, your next step should be getting to know your lead characters. Strong, unique characters are the secret to a movie's success. No matter what your story is, the events that construct it are happening to someone. And that someone better be interesting and, more importantly, must care about what is happening to and around them.

Pixar has created many unforgettable characters: The optimistic, amnesiac Dory; the mute, romantic Wall-E; snobbish critic Anton Ego; and, of course, deeply loyal toy cowboy Woody.

Why do these characters resonate so strongly? Well, they are all one of a kind. Pixar's commitment to exploring different worlds leads to a varied array of characters. Each of these characters enjoys a unique graphic design, representative of their unique attributes. (Ego especially manages to appear as snootiness incarnate.) They are given specific, unique traits, such as Dory's memory problems or Wall-E's infatuation with *Hello, Dolly!* These original, specific decisions are key to making main characters entertaining. But for them to compel an audience, you must also endow them with a deep passion for something…anything. We care because they care.

Woody cares deeply, almost obsessively, for Andy. Andy, as far as Woody can see, is his reason to live, and he takes great pride in being Andy's toy. This emotion is at the basis of every conflict Woody has throughout the series. It is why he is threatened by Buzz in *Toy Story*. It is why he gives up fame in a museum to return to Andy in *Toy Story 2*. It is what makes him manipulate Andy to give the toys to Bonnie at the end of *Toy Story 3* so that the toys can serve a new owner. Woody's belief that toys exist for their owner's enjoyment is tested again and again. This seems obvious, but it is calculated. If toys were indifferent to their owners or to whether they were played with, you wouldn't have much of a story. Woody wouldn't even mind that Andy tossed him aside in favor of Buzz. He'd retire happily. That is why the writers designed the toys to define themselves by their relationship with their owners. This isn't just true for Woody and the gang but also for Jessie and Lotso and practically every other toy presented. This deep dynamic is what makes the toys so interesting.

Woody's relationship with Andy and his desire to be played with are rooted in a firm set of beliefs about the role of a toy. Good characters care. Great characters care because they have strong opinions.

Strong Caring Stems from Strong Opinions

In *Brave*, Merida's mother, Elinor, cares deeply about, well, pretty much every little thing about Merida—her clothes, her hobbies, her manners, her voice projection, and most importantly, her imminent betrothal. Elinor has deep reasons for this nitpicky, annoying behavior. She believes that Merida's strength as a princess is the key to keeping the kingdom together and preventing a war like the one they had in the past. She honestly thinks that people can't escape the roles appointed to them, so it's best to be as prepared as possible to fulfill those roles. As Queen Elinor says, "We can't just run away from who we are." Elinor cares about Merida's manners because she has strong opinions about duty, diplomacy, and governing.

Why is this so important? Because it amplifies dramatic effect. Later in the movie, Merida rips her formal wear and shoots arrows—quite unlike a princess—and humiliates her suitors. As a mere act of teenage rebellion, this is interesting, but we've seen scores of teenage-rebellion scenes (though admittedly not in this setting). Merida and Elinor's deeply-held opinions transform the scene into a clash between ideas of freedom versus duty, and honest expression versus tactful diplomacy. These things mean a great deal more to the characters, and by proxy, to us.

As you can see from this example, strong opinions are fuel for conflict.

As a matter of fact, the plots and relationships in most of Pixar's films revolve around opposing opinions. In *Up*, Carl couldn't care less about Kevin, the rare exotic bird he encounters in Paradise Falls. However, he finds himself caught between Russell's adamant Boy Scout values of protecting nature and Muntz's belief that murder and cruelty are fine if that's what is needed to restore his reputation. These opposites force Carl to pick a side.

In *The Incredibles,* every character has a different idea about what it means to be incredible. Bob is bitter about a society that shuns exceptional people (superheroes) and longs to be able to express his (and his son's) outstanding talents. The film's main antagonist, Syndrome, wants to create a world in which exceptional abilities are available for everyone, thus eliminating the unique status of inherently gifted people, like the Incredibles. Their ideas drive the plot and propel it forward.

The Best Opinions Come from (Painful) Experience

Of course, opinions don't just manifest out of the ether. Think of your own opinions. They are most likely conclusions you have arrived at through your upbringing and years of education and experience. The same is true for your characters. You don't need to flash back to fifth grade to explain every attitude your character has, but strong opinions are often shaped by a character's past. It's even better if that past is rife with conflict and tension.

Almost all of Pixar's films present the past in a meaningful sequence: the lost commercials in *WallE*, Ego's flashback in *Ratatouille*, the prologues that begin *Up*, *Monsters University*, *The Incredibles*, and *Finding Nemo*. Often these glimpses of the past are used to provide texture and depth to a character's behavior.

Toy Story 2 and *Toy Story 3* construct long flashbacks that explain Jesse's and Lotso's distrust of human owners. In both cases, the heartbreak and betrayal they felt is brought vividly to life to make their present actions more intelligible and meaningful. Furthermore, it makes them more relatable and interesting. Take away Jessie's past, and she comes across as hateful and selfish. Adding a strong, dramatic reason for her behavior makes it hard to dismiss it as "bad" or "deluded." It makes her actions logical based on her experience, and by extension forces Woody to contend with her actions and attitudes on a deeper level and to be affected by them.

In *Cars*, the reveal of Doc Hudson's past as the Hudson Hornet is a major plot point. It changes McQueen's attitude toward him. It also explains Doc's deep disdain of the racing world that McQueen represents and adores.

Sometimes it takes only one line to give us all the background we need. In *The Incredibles,* Helen is vehemently opposed to Bob's attempts to relive his glory days. She thinks they should keep a low profile and not be outed as "supers." During their argument, she says, "It is a bad thing, Bob. Uprooting your family again." This single line implies the hardship they must have experienced in previously displacing their family and parting with friends, neighbors, schools, and jobs. This experience is the rationale behind her attitude, which pushes Bob to his secret visits to Syndrome's island, propelling the main plot of the film.

Common screenwriting lore often considers flashbacks as a tricky, treacherous tool that usually does more harm than good and should be avoided when possible. According to these "dry rules," many of Pixar's prologues should be jettisoned, especially considering that some of them are mostly expositional. However, these sequences work wonderfully, proving yet again that screenwriting rules should always be understood and examined rather than taken as blanket statements.

Pixar's flashbacks work so well because they are usually very economical, entertaining and well-placed. They usually occur at the beginning of the film, making them more of a prologue than a flashback, or they arrive organically as the story unfolds, as part of a character's action or reaction—for example, Ego's flashback at the dinner table, or Auto showing the lost file to the captain. Longer flashbacks succeed because Pixar treats them as independent short films, rather than as supplementary material for the main plot. *Up*'s prologue is complete on its own, with a full set of desires, obstacles, and turning points—all of which remain deeply linked to the main plot's goals and challenges.

Summary

Creating compelling characters is one of the biggest challenges you will face as a writer. You must use all your originality and insight to create a distinct and memorable individual whose story, appearance, and world are unique. Most importantly, your characters should care about ideas, values, and people, ideally out of a specific, opinionated point of view. When your characters' opinions are rooted in their experiences, especially painful experiences, it gives them depth and makes them more realistic. These three tools— passion, opinions, and experience—make the events in your story more meaningful and dramatic for your characters, and by proxy, for your audience.

In *Inside Out*

Like the toys in *Toy Story*, the emotions are deeply invested in Riley's well-being. The plot hinges on Joy's obsessive desire to keep Riley happy.

Experience also plays a crucial part in *Inside Out*. The film opens with the first time Joy made Riley happy. That is followed by Sadness's arrival, which causes Riley to cry and Joy to develop an opinion about Riley: she should always be happy. Furthermore, a major plot point revolves around one of Riley's own memories. Joy uses Riley's core hockey memory as an example of how important it is to make Riley happy. Later, when she realizes Sadness's crucial role in creating that memory, she sees her past in a different light, which forces her to change her opinions about how Headquarters should be run.

Do It Yourself: *Think about the characters in your story. What is important to them? What do they believe about love, friendship, death, freedom, and happiness? Why do they believe these things? How can you use their values and history to give the events of your plot a stronger impact on your characters?*

CHAPTER 3

CREATING EMPATHY

"But the thing that makes Woody special,
is he'll never give up on you... Ever.
He'll be there for you, no matter what."
—Andy

The Three Levels of Liking

What makes us like a movie character? Let's first examine what liking is. "Liking" comes in many shapes and forms. Go back to high school (only for a second, I promise). Who were the most popular kids? I'd bet that they were the most attractive and charismatic ones. That's one level on which you can "like" characters—for their obvious, external traits.

You probably like your friends for better reasons. They're fun and interesting to be with, they introduce you to new activities, ideas, or people you never knew. Perhaps they're just entertaining, or knowledgeable and passionate about something. Maybe they're funny or talented. That is the second level of engaging with a person or character. You learn more about their world and enjoy positive traits that require more discovery and attention than merely glancing at them.

Now think about how you became close with your very best friend.

When you first met, there were probably many moments of discovery, as you slowly learned their weird and amusing idiosyncrasies, until they turned into a unique person that only you really know. Some of those revelations were probably things the two of you had in common. Every time you discovered that this person shares your peeves, passions, goals, or beliefs, it brought you a little closer together. If the first two levels hinge mostly on positive or attractive traits, the third level can include less desirable aspects of a character. We forgive our friends their trespasses because we know them better and understand where they're coming from.

That's the third level of "liking," in which you become personally invested in the world of someone else to the point that their wins are your wins, and their losses are your losses. This level transcends the superficial fondness of the first two by allowing the audience to view the character as their proxy. The character becomes a surrogate for the audience's own hopes and fears. This is also called *empathy*, and it is crucial that your characters evoke it in your audience.

Empathy

You can use all three levels of "liking" when designing your characters. We take an immediate liking to Lightning McQueen at the beginning of *Cars,* as he charms us with his success and confidence. When we realize how self-centered he is, we quickly take a step back from his cocky demeanor, expecting him to change or evolve. Once in Radiator Falls, we start to suspect that there's more to him than meets the eye, and we lean in to witness his emotional journey.

The prologue of *The Incredibles* introduces us to Mr. Incredible and Elastigirl in the heyday of their success and fame. They're confident, sexy, and powerful. On top of that, we get a glimpse of the thrilling life of a superhuman crime fighter. But we don't see them just as perfect paragons. We watch as they flirt, as Bob is almost late to his own wedding. We witness smaller moments that bring us closer to them, rather than leaving us to admire them from afar.

Look at the character Wall-E, a mute waste-management robot—a far cry from your high school crush. We'd be hard pressed to describe Wall-E as charismatic. When we meet him, he's spending most of his time compacting garbage in a desolate wasteland. However, we quickly become privy to his hobbies and way of life.

As we follow him around, we see his commitment to his job, and the curiosity and meticulousness with which he collects relics from a lost world. We even get to see his obsession with *Hello, Dolly!* and his dreams of one day experiencing the emotions it depicts. Wall-E's coming-home ritual is something to which everyone can relate. He's simply returning home after a long day of work, indulging in his hobbies, and then plopping down in front of his favorite series. In between, he dreams about an exciting, one-of-a-kind love. What could be more familiar and intimate than that? It's the specificity and honesty of Wall-E's life that makes him so appealing.

The first layer of a character is easy to create but fades quickly. The third layer requires more details and originality, as well as more patience from your audience, but is more rewarding and creates a stronger bond with viewers. The second layer lies somewhere in between. You can coast on it for a long time, but without the substantial third layer, it won't resonate with your audience.

Empathy is a powerful phenomenon. Our ability to adopt the point of view of someone who seems completely different from us based on our shared core humanity is one of our distinctly human abilities. Use it wisely; the further you take us into the heart of someone completely different, the more rewarding and transformative our journey will be.

There's another method of creating empathy with a character, and arguably it is the most crucial: Place them in trouble. But remember that no one enjoys merely watching someone else suffer—simply tormenting your characters will cause more pity and aversion than empathy. Instead, characters should be placed in harm's way and then forced to bravely chart their course out of it.

Desire and Motive

Empathy is about recognizing ourselves in someone else by getting to know their idiosyncrasies and life experiences. How can you express someone's inner world in a manner to which an audience can relate? One way is to focus on a character's *desires*.

We all want things. They can be minute or grandiose, easily attainable or bordering on impossible. We spend most of our time chasing the things we want (an In-N-Out Burger, enough money to pay the rent, love, success, and so on). When we see a character truly desire something, we almost immediately take their side and hope they obtain it. Why? Because we hope to have our goals met just like the character does. As mentioned, one of the most inviting qualities about Wall-E is his desire to experience love. Likewise, McQueen's dreams of the winning the Piston Cup are part of what keeps us rooting for him despite his faults. When he finds himself stuck in Radiator Springs, with his lifelong dream in danger of slipping away, we relate to his frustration.

It's not enough to know only what a character wants. As storytellers, we must also know (and convey) *why* they want it. Remy the rat is obsessed with the human world. He wants to read, cook, and taste. He is inspired by humans and their ability to create and wants to be a creative cook, like his human hero, Gusteau. He wants these things despite the ridicule of his father, the misunderstanding of his friends, and the mortal danger involved in every trip to a human kitchen. Why? Remy is so motivated because he was born different, with an evolved sense of smell and taste. This gift makes Remy an outsider. His fellow rats don't know how to handle his uniqueness and instead chastise him for his peculiarities and exploit his gift for their own purposes by turning him into their poison checker. Naturally, Remy would feel driven to search for a place where he and his gifted talents might fit in better.

This is especially important when designing antagonistic characters.

Consider Henry J. Waternoose, the boss at Monsters, Inc. He condones the torture of Boo because he is desperate to find ways to create more energy for Monstropolis. Waternoose is burdened with the responsibility of keeping Monstropolis running. This desperate motivation causes him to do terrible things.

"When Remedies Are Past, the Griefs Are Ended"

In this quote from *Othello*, Shakespeare means to say that once there is no action left to take against an unfortunate event, then there is no point in being saddened by it anymore. Your characters should feel grief when they meet adversity, and that grief must last until remedies are past. Simply put, a character can give up and accept their fate only after every imaginable course of action has been tried.

Imagine this extremely unsatisfying version of *Finding Nemo*: Marlin's only son, Nemo, is kidnapped by scuba divers. Marlin chases the boat for about 10 minutes. As the boat motors out of sight, Marlin gives up, figuring it's hopeless, and goes back to the reef. The rest of the movie features Marlin crying over his bad luck. Not only is that version not exciting, it doesn't make us like Marlin very much. What father gives up on his son so easily? And why doesn't he do something about his loss, instead of whining?

Movie characters should have flaws, but among those flaws you'll almost never find defeatism. The characters in Pixar's films never give up. They will look death in the eye; they will conquer their deepest fears; they will change and adapt, if doing so offers a chance for them to get what they want. This is part of why Pixar's films are so satisfying. It's why you must design a strong reason for your character's desire. This motivation must be powerful enough to propel them through many trials.

Again, this relates to our identification with the character. We wish to live life this way, implacably following our desires. But we usually don't. Movies show us the risks and rewards, the trials and joys, of those who do.

This isn't to say that movie characters can't give up. As a matter of fact, they practically must give up—for a moment. In *A Bug's Life*, Flik accepts the worst perception of himself—a failure—before

Dot and the circus bugs rekindle his confidence. In *Finding Nemo,* even Marlin has a moment of complete hopelessness within the bowels of the whale, before being spouted out in Nemo's vicinity. Characters must experience these dark moments, because a character devoid of self-doubt and fear is unrelatable. Such a character simply isn't realistic. We know these emotions exist within us all, even the bravest and most successful of us, so they must exist within our characters as well.

Usually, Pixar's protagonists do go to the ends of the earth and get what they wanted, but not always. Mike Wazowski of *Monsters University* very badly wants to be a Scarer. He is so confident that he can be one that he ignores the many signs indicating that he just might not have it in him. Yet he never gives up. After he is kicked out of the scare program and stung by the lack of faith of his friends, he resorts to one last extreme attempt. Mike tries to face real humans on his own, breaking every rule in the monster world and believing he is risking his life. After failing to scare little children, he must face the truth: He simply isn't scary. It is important that Mike gives up only after he has tried everything imaginable (by himself, the writers, and the audience). A character that gives up easily frustrates an audience. A character that suffers a true, earned failure will resonate strongly with anyone invested in their quest.

There are many ways for a protagonist to demonstrate their determination—a character's journey isn't measured in miles, but in painful experiences and overcoming obstacles. In *Brave,*

Merida doesn't face many epic challenges. She spends most of the movie with the bear formerly known as her mother. Merida teaches her how to be a bear and devises a way to transform her to a human again. Unlike Marlin or Wall-E, Merida doesn't face endless physical antagonists. She needs to figure out how to reverse the spell, keep her father from killing her bear mother, and try not to get killed by Mordu. These obstacles are crucial, in the sense that they threaten her and her mother's lives, but they are peripheral to her main and self-proclaimed goal—to change her fate.

To change her fate, Merida must both learn from and teach her mother. She must shed some of her pride and learn to work together with Elinor. She needs to simultaneously earn her mother's trust and learn to forgive her. This isn't easy. Some family members lose touch for years because of their relatives' inability to evolve, forgive, communicate, and learn. To increase the stakes, her mother's predicament is Merida's own fault, indebting her with a lifetime of guilt and regret.

Merida's determination isn't measured only by the physical challenges she faces. It is tested by her ability to accept and negotiate her role as princess with her individuality, her values with her mother's, her passion with her duty, and her pride with her empathy. Only after Merida successfully navigates these waters in front of the three kingdoms does she learn respect for her mother's ways. That is what allows her to conjure up the love and forgiveness that makes Elinor human again.

Merida had to search deep within herself, discover qualities she didn't think she had—that she disdained, even—to reverse her mistake and truly change her fate, and that of the kingdom's, for the better.

Summary

For the audience to transcend from liking your characters to empathizing with them, you must create rich, specific characters. Through a process of discovery, you must dole out the idiosyncrasies of your fictional creations while highlighting what is relatable, human, and universal about them. One of the most universal things is desire. Giving your character a clear goal and a strong motivation behind it will help people empathize with your character, even when their actions are questionable. Lastly, while pursuing their goals, characters should be bold and determined, bravely battling their self-doubt, and never giving up until they have done everything imaginable to achieve their goal.

In *Inside Out*

Joy is immediately likable. Not only is she cheerful and literally glowing, she is happiness incarnate. Her entire purpose in life is to make someone happy. The opening quickly familiarizes us with her surroundings so we can feel comfortable with them and with her. Once she and Sadness find themselves outside of Headquarters, a clear and urgent goal is introduced: Bring the core emotions back where they belong so Riley's Islands of Personality don't collapse. This makes the audience empathize with her even more. Together with Sadness and Bing Bong, Joy navigates the dangerous, life-threatening terrain of Riley's mind, not letting anything discourage her from setting things right.

Bing Bong deserves a special mention here. We meet him pathetically stealing memories from his time with Riley. We forgive this trespass because he has a strong, relatable motivation: He is forgotten and discarded. Everyone has felt like that at some point. Yet despite his pain, Bing Bong's main directive is still Riley's well-being, which is why he helps Joy and Sadness in their dangerous quest. He is so dedicated to this objective, that he even sacrifices himself, giving up on ever being remembered again, so Riley will have a chance of being happy again. That is a determined character.

Do It Yourself: *How do you feel about the characters in your story? Are they unique or generic? Do they have habits, hobbies, or routines that make them feel real and specific? Do they have a clear goal or a campaign that an audience can get behind? Is the reason for pursuing this goal strong and fleshed out? In pursuit of this goal, how hard and far do characters push themselves? Do they go to great lengths or merely try half-heartedly? Are their challenges external and physical, or interpersonal and emotional?*

CHAPTER 4

DRAMA AND CONFLICT

"Well, if you hadn't shown up
in your stupid little cardboard spaceship and
taken away everything that was important to me..."
—Woody

More Than Life and Death

It is common knowledge that films thrive on conflict. It seems to me that conflict is often narrowly interpreted. Conflict is much more comprehensive than an asteroid hurtling toward Earth or two people arguing. One broader way to define conflict is as the obstacles that stand between your protagonist and their goal. The more unique, original, and layered these obstacles are, the more your story will stand out and satisfy your audience.

Pixar has moments of physical, life-or-death moments in practically all their films. You'd expect the superheroes in *The Incredibles* and the ruthless worlds of insects and sea life in *A Bug's Life* and *Finding Nemo,* respectively, to have these kinds of moments, but Pixar finds ways to infuse the danger of irreversible physical harm into all its films. *Up* may be the story of a widower who learns to live his life after his love has passed away, but the film leads him into daring duels with a megalomaniac aboard a zeppelin. In the universe of *Monsters, Inc.* and *Monsters University,* it is believed that the mere touch of a human will kill a monster. Even if this is a fallacy, the rules and organizations that evolve around it create strong conflict at every step of the way—and that's before even mentioning the nefarious Randal Boggs. *Cars* is the closest Pixar came to a film without life-or-death moments. Only in the two races that bookend the film are the cars in any real existential danger.

Fighting for their life is the biggest conflict a character can face, as death is an insurmountable obstacle to all goals a character might have. This is something writers can use, especially when depicting dangerous worlds. Eve could've entered Wall-E's life by slowly floating down from the sky. Instead, she enters inside an enormous spaceship with immense burners that threaten to incinerate Wall-E unless he finds a way to hide from them in time. However, this choice is in no way crucial to the story. *Wall-E* would've been essentially the same film with both entrances. But choosing a more dangerous one creates one more moment of drama, one more gasp from the audience of "Will he make it?"—and audiences love to gasp. So, if your setting offers opportunities for such moments, mine them.

Keep in mind that life-threatening situations are just a starting point. Death is an obstacle to all goals, but merely living is a dull goal. Designing specific, personal goals for your protagonists, based on their opinions and desires, can lead you toward more interesting conflicts that you should develop and explore.

Another way to define conflict is as a situation in which two opposite forces struggle with each other. This means that every conflict has a built-in question: Who will win? While this view pertains to the physical conflicts, it is particularly useful when discussing internal conflicts.

As mentioned in the first chapter, opinions are fuel for conflict. Once a character cares deeply about something, you can create powerful, emotional conflict surrounding that emotion. Conflicts rooted in a character's opinions and emotions are a little harder to convey, both because they exist in a character's mind, and because they are more specific and less universal than life or death. They require deeper understanding of the character and world you've created. You must explain the emotional constitution that allows your character to have these opinions. (This explanation is more formally known as "exposition.") Furthermore, you must highlight the submerged conflict question, the two forces at play.

For example, the question presented at the beginning of *Up* is "Will Carl find a new sense of purpose in life?" How is this question presented? By the juxtaposition of the vibrant life and dreams he shared with Ellie with the gray, dull, meaningless life he is living in the wake of her death. In a way, stories are a series of conflict-questions presented and answered. Some deal with external forces and some with internal forces.

Creating and Communicating Emotional Conflict

Conflict is more effective when there is something your character is risking. This is where the opinions we discussed in the first chapter come in.

Your characters must care about something. When they stand to lose that something, you have conflict. Consider Woody's dilemma in *Toy Story 2*. Upon discovering that he is part of a collector's series, Woody is about to face a lifetime in a museum. At first this sounds terrible, but as he grows close to his new companions and contemplates an eternity of being looked at and appreciated, he begins to consider it. When Buzz and his friends come to bring Woody back home to Andy, he isn't sure what he should do. After hearing Jesse's story about being discarded by her owner, and Woody's own brush with being forgotten and "put on the shelf," he doesn't have much confidence in his future with Andy. Buzz reminds him of the values Woody himself taught the spaceman about loyalty to the kid who loves you. This belief is at Woody's core. However, the fear he faces because of his injury and being placed on the shelf gets the better of him. He refuses to return to Andy and opts for the museum.

What is the conflict in this scene? Superficially, the conflict is between Woody and Buzz. Buzz wants Woody to come home; Woody doesn't want to come home. There are opposing forces, and a dramatic question arises ("Will Woody come home?"). But there is a deeper conflict occurring here. Woody has a goal. He wants to mean something to someone. That has been his goal in *Toy Story* (where Buzz is an obstacle to achieving that goal) and will be again in *Toy Story 3* (where Woody achieves this goal by becoming the plaything of a younger child). He is torn by two opposing forces that will determine how he will go about achieving this goal. On one hand is his devotion to Andy and core belief that toys should be loyal to their children. On the other hand is his fear of being discarded by Andy, either because of wear and tear or just because Andy will grow tired of him. The inner-conflict question would be, "Will Woody stay loyal to Andy or succumb to his fears and opt for a safer life in a museum?"

At first, Woody's fears win out, but as "You've Got a Friend in Me" plays on the TV and Woody scratches the sole of his shoe to see Andy's name, his sense of loyalty comes through, and he decides to return to his owner. The trick in this scene is to find external, filmable ways to present Woody's inner conflict. Buzz, the song, and the name on his shoe represent his loyalty. His dialogue and Jesse and the Roundup Gang represent his fear.

Making the Stakes Real and Larger Than Life

Pixar's films deal with extremes. This means that no matter what the stakes are, Pixar will amplify them as much as possible.

Most love stories revolve around finding, winning over, and holding on to the love of your life. Usually, should a character fail to succeed in this, we know they will be miserable, but we also know it's likely that after a while, they will find someone else. In Pixar's only film that is predominantly a love story, *Wall-E,* the stakes are significantly higher. If Wall-E doesn't win Eve's heart, he will remain alone. But this is loneliness with a capital L. We're talking about remaining as the only sentient being on the planet, talking to a cockroach and watching the same movie over and over forever. It's not just about some guy losing a girl. It's about remaining alone in the universe. If that's not amplified enough, consider the events that occur later in the film as the focal genre switches to dystopian sci-fi, and the entire future of humanity is in danger.

Extremes can also be found in more modest settings, such as a French restaurant. The climax of *Ratatouille* revolves around the visit of influential critic Anton Ego to Gusteau's restaurant. For this conflict to be interesting, the stakes need to be high: Ego must have true and complete destructive capability over Remy and Linguini. Making him the toughest and most respected food critic in Paris is a nice start. But consider how he is introduced at the beginning of the film. He is given the title "The Grim Eater," and it was his scathing review that cost

Gusteau's restaurant a star and seems to have caused Gusteau's untimely death. His title and his review both depict him as someone with the power to destroy a life.

After the restaurant's staff leaves, except for Collette and Linguini, this is Remy's last chance to prove he is indeed a rat who can cook. Ego can either validate that or destroy Remy's dreams for good, in the same way that Woody's choice to go to the museum would have destroyed his relationship with Andy, and hence his loyalty and self-perception for good.

Exposing and Changing Characters—A Chance at Construction

Conflict is needed because, well, audiences find it enjoyable. They are presented with two opposing forces and want to know which will win—very much like spectator sports, which have entertained masses since the dawn of time (except that movies come with a much better chance that your favorite will win). Pixar's films usually offer something more in this struggle. In their movies, conflict tends to expose or change something emotional within the core of their characters.

This is the flip side of the destructive force mentioned earlier. Characters must be in danger of destruction, but they must also have a chance at *construction* as well. They must stand a chance of surviving the threat they're facing, and of emerging from the struggle stronger and whole—perhaps defeating the flaw mentioned earlier. If a force is defeated but the protagonist remains susceptible to the same form and strength of attack again, then they haven't truly defeated that force. Furthermore, the movie would feel futile.

At the beginning of *A Bug's Life*, the colony is forced to create an offering of food for the grasshoppers or else be destroyed by them. When their offering is ruined, the colony focuses on finding more food so the grasshoppers will spare them. Only Flik tries to find a way to get rid of the grasshoppers *for good*. As the colony fails to meet the quota and Flik's initial plan fails to expel the grasshoppers, the destruction of the colony becomes imminent. The grasshoppers have moved in and have enslaved the colony, and Hopper, their ruthless leader, plans to kill the queen. This situation is partially a result of Flik's attempts at changing the colony and changing the status quo— his attempts at construction.

By the end of the film, Flik manages to change the entire perception of both ants and grasshoppers, as the countless ants realize their power and band together to fight their oppressors, driving them out of the colony. Flik also succeeds in killing Hopper, the grasshoppers' leader. Had the movie ended with the colony merely appeasing the grasshoppers with a new offering, there would be no chance or attempt at construction. We would leave the film knowing that the grasshoppers will return the following winter and that the chain of events we were so involved in would likely repeat itself. That wouldn't make for a very satisfying experience.

In storytelling, the most powerful instance of construction is personal, when a protagonist must change something deep within themselves to achieve their goal. This is deeply moving because true change is extremely hard to achieve—in fiction and in life. We resist change, and so do our characters, because change entails risk. Did you ever try to kick a bad habit? Or embark on some new venture? Change doesn't just bring with it a new, unknown territory and the risk of ridicule or failure—it also forces us to dismantle some part of us. Every change isn't just a birth but also a death, as characters must part with some deep aspect of themselves.

In *Toy Story 3,* Woody and the toys are still in the same state of mind they had been in in the previous films. Their core desire is still to be played with, and they are deeply devoted to Andy. Therefore, they succumb to a life in the attic. Woody knows his glory days with Andy are gone, but he still hopes to escort him to college and be a part of his life. By the end of the film, these perceptions change. The toys still crave mattering to a child, but they accept the end of their relationship with Andy. After spending three movies watching these characters' obsessive devotion to Andy, seeing them voluntarily part with him is practically earth-shattering. Woody's choice, to have Andy give him away to a younger girl rather than take him to college, is one he never would have made at the beginning of the film. The toys' ordeals, and their encounters with Lotso and Bonnie, allow them to realize that it's okay to let go. Andy has moved on, and so should they. This allows them to achieve their goal, but in a way they never would have dreamed. Notice how this change is both death and birth: Yes, the toys found a new home that seems to solve all their problems, but this solution forces them to leave their cherished owner, Andy. Change always comes with a price.

This means a protagonist's goal might change throughout your story.

McQueen's desire for almost the duration of *Cars* is winning the Piston Cup. Slowly, a new desire emerges: to become a reliable member of a community. For the first time in his life, he wants to be part of a group, but that group won't accept him if he remains the egotistical, vain car that he is. By the end of the film, he must choose between these two desires, and McQueen chooses the new one, giving up on winning the Piston Cup. This change wouldn't have been possible (or plausible) without the conflict he faced throughout the film.

If the conflict in your story merely allows your character to show their skills, or to stretch them, you're only halfway there. Try cranking up the discomfort, forcing your characters to dispense with whatever baggage is hindering them, and build themselves anew, to deal with the threats you've created.

Summary

Conflict is a collision of two opposing forces, which offers a dramatic question to an audience: "Which force will win?" Pixar's films often depict dangerous worlds rife with life-and-death situations, where losing the struggle would mean the demise of a protagonist. While these conflicts are entertaining and easily relatable, Pixar strives to create deep emotional effects on its audience. To achieve them, they create strong internal conflicts.

These kinds of conflicts are challenging to create and communicate. They must be rooted in the opinions and beliefs of a character and must put them in danger of losing something dear, usually a part of their identity. To express the emotional forces struggling within, we must find filmable, external expressions of the conflicts: other characters, mementos, dialogue, or a symbol system that is clear to the audience. Making the situation extreme also helps convey the meaning of your character's struggle.

The best kind of conflict offers a chance for both destruction and construction, which would have a fortifying effect against the antagonistic forces. Construction can only come from change, to which characters and people are naturally averse. Therefore, the quality of the conflict in your script is measured by the believable change it propels in your characters. Change is the measuring unit of conflict.

In *Inside Out*

Inside Out has a very sly set of stakes. By clearly setting up the meaning and structure of Riley's mindscape, *Inside Out* also introduces potential risks. The Islands of Personality are "what makes Riley, Riley." Joy is what makes Riley happy. Without her, Riley can't feel joy. This creates a smart conflict-efficient connection between Riley's emotional journey and the emotions' physical, life-or-death situations. When Riley steals money from her parents, Honesty Island crumbles apart, almost killing Joy, Sadness, and Bing Bong. What better way to externalize inner conflicts than setting your story inside your character's mind?

Of course, our protagonists risk more than their lives. Bing Bong's fear of being forgotten goes far beyond a simple fear of death. It is the complete removal of his bond with Riley, his sole purpose in life, that frightens him.

Bing Bong cares more about Riley remembering him and their happy times together than his own personal existence. This added layer of consequence is part of what makes Bing Bong's character arc so poignant.

Pixar also wisely exacerbates smaller conflicts by manipulating expectations. The emotions' fantasies and expectations for Riley's new house are so pleasant and outrageous that they make the disappointment at the drab house she arrives at have a bigger impact on the audience. Before springing something good or bad on your characters and audience, set opposite expectations for a stronger effect.

Inside Out is also very smart about the forces of destruction and construction in play. At first, it seems the biggest danger is Riley being sad. Once the core memories are misplaced, Riley's Islands of Personality start to crumble, threatening the very core of who she is (a beautiful visual metaphor).

Inside Out saves its most fatal attack for the very end of the film. In a shrewd metaphor for depression, the controls in the command center go numb and unresponsive, as Riley stops feeling anything. This is the worst thing that could happen to our heroes, the emotions: No one can feel them anymore—the film's point here being that numbness is much worse than being ruled by your anger, fear, or disgust. Construction comes in the form of the new shared memories. Pixar crafts a very potent image of the shelves of memories, each of them now tinted with two colors or more, signaling the new cooperation between the emotions. In addition, several new Islands of Personality have been constructed, and the emotions now work with a new, bigger control panel, signaling Riley's emotional growth.

Do It Yourself: *What is the main dramatic question in your script? What is the answer the audience must stick around to see? Does this question have an emotional component? Have you found an original, organic way of expressing this inner struggle in the physical world of your story? Is there a force capable of destroying your characters? Is there a force in your story capable of pushing the characters to construct something new and stronger? Do your characters change in a clear, discernible way because of the conflicts they face?*

CHAPTER 5

PIXAR'S STRUCTURE

*"Just like a movie! The robot will
emerge dramatically, do some damage,
throw some screaming people, and just when
all hope is lost, Syndrome will save the day!
I'll be a bigger hero than you ever were!"*
—Syndrome

A Word on Structure

Structure is one of the most hotly debated aspects of screenwriting. For centuries, writers and scholars have suggested myriad forms for narrative structure, but I will not delve into these many different and useful models here.

A structure's goal is to serve as a road map for your writing, creating a series of suggested goalposts to help you both construct and analyze your story. Because various structures can work, no single structure is considered gospel. Not every story you write will fit an existing structure in every way. And that is perfectly fine. These structures are tools you can use to diagnose your work or use as buoys to help navigate the murky waters of your developing story.

Different theories of structure share a similar core. The most ubiquitous structure, honed down to the basic concepts that most theorists agree on, has the following characteristics:

Three parts: the beginning, middle, and end. The middle will be longest and will focus on obstacles. The first part focuses on giving needed information to the viewer (exposition). In our terms, the beginning is needed to show a character's comfort zone (or what Christopher Vogler calls the Ordinary World) so that we can appreciate their discomfort when they are forced to leave it. The ending resolves the dramatic questions presented and tends to be a little shorter than the beginning and rhythmically quicker (with shorter scenes and the convergence of plot lines).

A satisfying story will usually have between three and five major events. While different theories give these events different names, they have become so common and useful that every writer should know their aliases. The first event is known as the "inciting incident." It is the first meaningful event to happen in your story. It takes place in act one and begins the plot and propels your protagonist to act: Nemo is kidnapped; Flik destroys the offering.

The second event is known as the "first plot point." It often cements the protagonist's commitment to their quest and serves as an inciting incident of sorts for the second act, sending our hero in a new direction. Marlin finds the address of the scuba diver and heads for Sydney, Australia; In *Toy Story 3*, the toys discover they are captives in daycare hell. The first plot point usually happens around the quarter mark of the film. Sometimes it converges with the inciting incident.

The third major event is the "second plot point," which takes place around the three-quarter mark of the film. The second plot point will usually feature a strong blow to our protagonists and will set up the third act: Marlin believes Nemo is dead; Auto takes over the ship and gets rid of Wall-E and Eve.

The last major event is the "climax" of your story. The climax should be a suspenseful, grand scene rife with conflict that answers the main dramatic question of your story. It will usually take place several minutes before the end of your film: Marlin allows Nemo to use what he learned to save Dory and the guppies; Anton Ego comes to dine.

Some theories include an additional major event that takes place at the midpoint of the film.

The best way to think of plot points is as a combination of an inciting incident and a climax. The inciting incident begins a story, raises dramatic questions, and sends a character on a journey. The climax answers dramatic questions and features a tense, potent moment of conflict, which is resolved in a satisfying manner. Plot points must do both. They must set your hero on a new path while also resolving some of the dramatic questions already raised—though never *the* dramatic question of your story. Because plot points are a combination of inciting incident and climax, they aren't as potent a catalyst as the former nor as final a resolution as the latter.

The position of these events isn't exact science. Yes, the markers described above seem to work well. However, even a cursory look at Pixar's films show that structure can be played with. In *Monsters, Inc.,* the first major event comes about 23 minutes in, when Sully finds Boo, a human child who has escaped into the monster world. In *A Bug's Life,* the first major event comes 9 minutes in, when Flik destroys the offering for the grasshoppers. In *The Incredibles,* Bob receives the message inviting him to a secret island, thus setting in motion the film's main plot, 30 minutes in.

Clearly, all three of these movies are great films. Use structures to help you figure out what works for your film—and not the other way around.

The main point to take from this section is that stories require a setup, a series of trials and a resolution. They also seem to require at least three major events—three major clashes of opposing forces that usually result in a major decision by your protagonist. Pixar's films seem to include more than three.

Let's explore their structures further.

Major Events—Whats, Hows, and Whys

One way to think of major events is as the "what happens" of your story, connected by the "hows" and "whys." For example, the first plot point in *Up* is Carl's decision to tie a lot of balloons to his house and fly to Paradise Falls. Everything before that is about why and how he does it. It is important that these "hows" and "whys" keep conflict in play and keep the audience cognizant of the opposing forces threatening your protagonists.

The major events in *Finding Nemo* could be described as follows: Marlin's son Nemo is kidnapped by scuba divers (inciting incident); Marlin finds a clue and sets out to find Nemo (plot point one); Marlin gives up after thinking his son is dead (plot point two); Marlin and Nemo reunite, resolve their emotional issues, and save Dory and the guppies (climax). Notice that each of these descriptions begs questions: Why does Marlin give up? How did he come to think that his son is dead? Why is he so determined to find Nemo? How does he find the faraway land of Sydney, Australia? The "whys" are answered by exposition, and the "hows" by scenes of activity.

What differentiates these four major moments from the rest of the film? They aren't necessarily the most exciting moments. Marlin is chased by sharks, miraculously survives a sea of jellyfish, and makes his way out of a whale's stomach. One way to consider these moments is to think about how they relate to the *existing flaw* we saw at the beginning of the movie.

More specifically, they must both either offer a chance to fix it or a chance to destroy all hope of fixing it (destruction or construction), forcing the protagonist to plough ahead or be destroyed. It's like the increments on "Who Wants to be a Millionaire?" Marlin could give up after finding the address—deciding that Sydney is too far and that he could never reach it, thus succumbing to his flaw (anxiety) and giving up hope of fixing it for the sake of his son. Major events are crossroads, which usually offer a chance for a character to cut their losses or continue bravely ahead.

If we start with Marlin as an overprotective father living in the shadow of losing his entire family, then these events connect directly with his existing problem: He loses his last progeny; he gets hope of finding him; he loses hope of finding him; he finds him. These moments connect directly with Marlin's chance at the destruction or construction of his existing flaw (having his worst fear come true, or overcoming his worst fear and learning to manage his fears and create a healthier relationship with his son). Whether Marlin will escape killer sharks is clearly relevant—dead fish can't find anyone—but doesn't pertain directly to the main dramatic question. Major events—the inciting incident, plot points, and climax—pertain to the main dramatic question.

If most scenes in your script deal with overcoming obstacles, major events are often about revising goals, perceptions, and strategies. In *Cars,* the first major event (McQueen is stuck in

Radiator Springs), changes his goal from winning the Piston cup to escaping Radiator Springs (in time to win the Piston Cup). The second plot point is when McQueen is found and brought back to the racing world, putting him on track for the Piston Cup. However, by this point he is a different character with different values that he exhibits in the next major event—the climax—when he chooses acting in grace and comradery over winning the cup.

Pixar creates more plot points and major events than it initially seems. The writers use subplots, parallel plots, and internal plots to create more stories and thus more major events. This story inflation seems to keep the audience's interest and satisfy them emotionally and narratively.

A Multilayered Storytelling Cake

Let's reexamine *Finding Nemo*. We mentioned four major events that all pertain to Marlin's search: losing Nemo, finding a clue, giving up, and reuniting. However, the movie has many more narrative threads. We have Marlin and Dory's relationship, Nemo's new friends and escape plan, and Marlin's inner transition from neurotic fish and father to a brave adventurous soul.

Each of these plots comes with its own set of major events. (Practically every scene in Nemo's aquarium serves as a major event in his story).

Pixar's films aren't the only ones that have a multilayered set of subplots that create many meaningful turns, but it does seem that Pixar cracked the code as to how these subplots should relate to one another. The main plot should be epic, adventurous, and rife with action, with an emphasis on life-or-death, physical situations. (A father searches the ocean! A robot must travel through space to bring mankind back to earth!) Under that main plot, there will be an emotional, internal story. (A father must deal with past trauma and give his son space; a rat must come to terms with conflicting parts of his identity.) All the studio's stories also feature a major, complex bonding process with another equally flawed character from a different world. (A nervous father bonds with a carefree, memory-impaired fish; a monster bonds with a terrified human child who he believes can kill him.) Sometimes Pixar will add another subplot, usually taking place parallel to the main plot. (Nemo tries to escape his tank; Skinner tries to rob Linguini out of inheriting Gusteau's estate.)

This triple and sometimes quadruple structure seems to satisfy all the reasons we go to the movies: high-end adventure, meaningful relationships, and deep emotional struggles. Pixar's skill in juggling these layers, and threading them together strongly, seamlessly, and honestly is what sets them apart. The different layers reinforce one another, giving emotional weight to the daring actions and clear dramatic expression to the emotional conflicts.

Bonding Stories

As mentioned, conflict is crucial to your story and, yes, there is something deeply satisfying about watching a character fight against the odds for something they deeply believe in. But it is also very satisfying to watch two characters from different worlds grow closer together and balm each other's wounds— when it is earned. By "earned," I'm referring to a believable, specific process of bonding. Watching two people meet and immediately become best friends isn't moving. Nor is watching two people hate each other for an entire movie, only to turn on a dime and fall in love in the last minutes of the film.

Bonding should involve two characters who have clear reasons not to like each other. Only through a parallel process of external events pushing them together *and* inner changes that remove the relationship's emotional obstacles, can they come together in a way that is truly meaningful.

Take Woody and Buzz, for example. Initially, they are nothing but a threat to each other. Woody hates Buzz because he is a direct threat to his relationship with Andy, which is at the core of Woody's existence. Buzz can't truly befriend Woody because he insists that Zurg and Star Command don't exist and that Buzz is "just a toy"—thus threatening the core of his existence. It is only after Buzz fails to fly and Woody accepts his transiency as a toy that they start to cooperate. They are forced to work together to escape Sid's basement. Only in the very last minute of *Toy Story* are they presented as truly bonded, when they both listen in on Andy unwrapping his new birthday presents.

Sometimes bonding is propelled by discoveries about the other characters. In *Cars,* McQueen is much more interested in what Doc Hudson has to say after Doc beats him at a race, and he's even more interested after he discovers Doc's old Piston Cups. Sometimes it is a self-discovery: In *Monster's Inc.,* Sully grows that much closer to Boo after she is terrified by his performance at the simulator. As he examines monstrous photos of himself, he realizes for the first time the fear human children feel when he scares them. This understanding brings him closer to Boo.

Double Climaxes

Many of Pixar's films feature a double climax. The main story is resolved in a grand, high-stakes sequence, as in most films. In Pixar's films, this storytelling peak is usually followed by a quieter climax scene, designed to resolve one of the more internal stories.

Nowhere is this clearer than in *Toy Story 3*. After a harrowing sequence in a dump's incinerator, the toys have both narrowly escaped death and gotten rid of Lotso. They are free to do as they please—head back home to Andy, or search for greener pastures. All the prison-escaping, villain-fighting, almost-getting-burned-to-death parts of the film have been resolved, yet there are 15 minutes left. The film memorably turns to its internal narratives for these final moving moments.

The toys head back to Andy's place. Woody takes his place with Andy's college things as the rest of the toys prepare to spend the rest of their life in a box. After spending an entire film feeling betrayed by Andy, the toys now accept their place in the attic. Woody spent *Toy Story 3* fighting to free his friends so they could all return to be with Andy, fulfilling their position as toys in any way Andy sees fit. However, after his journey, Woody sees another solution.

He tricks Andy into donating all the toys, including himself, to Bonnie. This decision powerfully resolves three movies' worth of relationships. Woody accepts the conclusion of his role in Andy's life yet doesn't succumb to a life in the attic. Who said a toy should have only one owner? He and the rest of the gang get to start over, with many hours of playtime ahead. Andy accepts the end of childhood and parts with his toys, but not before acknowledging the meaning they had in his life and proving that they will always be a part of him.

Another clear example can be found in *Up*. After a hair-raising chase and fight aboard a zeppelin, Muntz is defeated and our heroes are safe. The audience can finally breathe again. But before they do, Carl and Russel watch as Carl's treasured house, the one he fiercely defended from harm throughout their journey, floats away into the sky. Russel offers his sympathy, but Carl simply replies "It's just a house." This little moment resolves Carl's inner conflict of letting go of Ellie and his previous life and embracing a new one. It happens subtly, straight on the heels of the action climax.

Don't Abuse Structure

This structure, and probably any other one, can easily be abused. A blunt and technical insertion of an element into your story will only make your script worse. This isn't a to-do list where you must check off items. These are useful elements to be implemented with care. Don't force a "bonding process" into your script if it doesn't call for one. That's not the Pixar way.

Most of Pixar's bonding stories are the main plot of their film, enhanced by the adventure sequences. *Brave* is much more about a mother and daughter who learn to understand each other than it is about bears and witches. In *Cars*, McQueen spends a lot more time with new friends in Radiator Springs than on the racetrack. In *Toy Story*, the main relationship is essential to its plot, which revolves around Woody and Buzz's relationship.

Sometimes Pixar introduces journey buddies who aren't inherent to the core of the film's story, such as in *Up* and *Finding Nemo*. They make these additions feel natural and pertinent through meticulous character design. Russel and Dory are constructed so that they will push the plot forward when Carl and Marlin can't. They are endowed with points of view that clash with those of Carl and Marlin. Russel's Boy Scout values and sense of adventure are a foil for Carl's reclusiveness and lack of purpose. The same goes for Dory's eternal optimism and confidence, which contrast Marlin's anxiety. Pixar goes a step further by creating an inner world and existing flaw for these characters. Russel is lonely and feels estranged from and rejected by his father. Dory can't remember anything for more than a minute or so, which causes her to live a lonely life. Let's not forget that Pixar also makes both characters incredibly funny.

Whenever you're adding an element to your story, make sure it's inherent in your original concept. Try to explore and expand existing characters, settings, plots, and themes. If you're adding a more external element, take extra care to develop it in a way that interacts meaningfully with your core characters and story.

Summary

There are many forms of structure. Most agree on the three parts of story: setup, trials, and climax and resolution. They also focus on the major events stories must have: one to start it, one to end it and one to three more in between. These events are integral parts of the main story of your film, and each pertains directly to your protagonist's main problem. They are what happens in your story, whereas the scenes around them depict how and why they happen.

Pixar's films usually have a layered structure that involves an adventurous life-or-death action story, an interpersonal story of bonding, and an inner emotional struggle. These layers are interconnected. This structure serves as a force multiplier, enriching each of these stories separately and creating more major events, which audiences seem to enjoy. Often,

Pixar's films will include yet another storyline, taking place concurrently with the main story.

This structure also results in a double climax, where Pixar stages a grand, suspenseful, awe-inspiring, life-or-death sequence—the climax of the film's main plot—which is followed by a moving emotional climax. This double whammy creates powerfully moving and satisfying endings.

In *Inside Out*

Inside Out contains four plots: The main, adventurous plot, in which Joy and Sadness must bring the core memories back to Headquarters before it's too late; the bonding plot between Joy and Sadness, which mirrors the plot of Riley's inner conflict to find the power to tell her parents that she can't be happy for them all the time; and last but not least, Bing Bong's moving subplot. While both Joy and Sadness change during the film, most of their inner journey is part of their bonding experience and is not an independent narrative thread. *Inside Out* adds a nice touch of elegance to Pixar's structure, as its unique premise promises that every small change in Riley's inner emotions will have devastating effects for the protagonists who live in her mind.

The inciting incident would be Riley's move to San Francisco, which summons Sadness into a more prominent role within Headquarters. Because of that, clashes begin between her and

Joy, which lead to the first plot point of them finding themselves outside of Headquarters, with the core memories urgently trying to bring them back. See how that almost feels like the beginning of a different movie? The second act is in a different environment, outside of Headquarters, and has a different goal. If you define Joy's desire as "Keeping Riley happy," you can see how the turning point affects that. In act one, Joy's goal was to keep Riley happy by limiting Sadness's influence (thus also setting up our bonding plot). In the second act, Joy's goal is to get back to Headquarters with the memories to keep Riley happy. During the second act, the emphasis shifts to the physical adventure plot as Joy braves the dangerous, uncharted world of Riley's mind.

A look at the film's second plot points shows how wisely and intricately Pixar balances the different layers mentioned. In Riley's story, this major event is her idea—prompted by Anger—to run away to Minnesota. This in turn causes the destruction of Honesty and Family Islands, stranding Joy along with the memories (main plot) and Bing Bong (subplot) in the Memory Dump, about to be forgotten—as far away from achieving their goals (keeping Riley happy and returning to prominence in Riley's mind, respectively) as they ever were. In between all the destruction, Pixar squeezes in a meaningful moment between Joy and Sadness (bonding plot), which is the nadir of their relationship, when Joy leaves Sadness alone and tries to return to Headquarters without her, essentially deeming her harmful and useless. All these events take place within a span of about 6 minutes, and each serves as the second plot point in a separate subplot.

In the third act, Joy makes her way back to the control room, bringing Sadness with her. The climax begins when Joy and Sadness arrive at Headquarters, almost too late. They must reverse the damage and get Riley out of her depression. Here Joy demonstrates her inner change and gives Sadness the gears, thus resolving both the bonding plot and the main dramatic question ("How will Riley and the emotions deal with the sadness of moving to San Francisco?"). Sadness demonstrates her newfound sense of purpose by confidently taking the gears and instinctively knowing that she and Joy can share them.

Do It Yourself: *Does your story feature all of Pixar's three layers? Do you have a high-stakes action plot with chases, set pieces (powerful scenes that are very exciting, emotional, original, elaborate, or otherwise memorable and grand), and life-or-death situations? Is there an honest bonding plot in your story? Is it deeply connected to the main story you're telling? Are the characters kept apart by conflicting points of view and emotional obstacles? Does your protagonist have an internal struggle they must resolve? Is that struggle strongly connected to your other stories? Is it dramatized externally through these other stories? Do each of these stories reach a climax in a strong, clear way, distinguishing them if necessary?*

CHAPTER 6

CASTING CHARACTERS

"I know his type. Race car. The
last thing this town needs."
—Doc Hudson

Your Story as an Efficient Machine

In Chapter 1, we explored how every moment in *Ratatouille* pertains to its core idea. This is true of all Pixar's films. They each feel like a complex mechanism, in which all parts work together efficiently. Where nothing is missing, nothing is redundant, and every element has a function.

Everything you introduce in your script—every line, character, theme, or piece of information—must have a function and be part of the grand scheme. Often, all this means is exploring how to make the most out of every preexisting element in your script. In *Finding Nemo*, Nemo finds himself stuck in an aquarium. Rather than leave it at that, Pixar takes special care to imbue this new setting with entertainment and meaning. Each character is distinctly designed and given some sort of comedic behavior. Gil, the dark and wounded fish that's planning escape, is given even more than that. He is pitted in opposition to Marlin. Gil urges Nemo to test his limits, even if it's risky. Gil's wounded fin creates a kinship between Nemo and Gil, and a parallel. Nemo was taught to think of himself as fragile and handicapped, but Gil refuses to acknowledge any impediment for Nemo or himself. Nemo learns self-worth and courage thanks to Gil's different take on his situation.

When casting the characters of *The Incredibles,* the writers made sure that each family member had a different take on their superpowers. Bob misses his glory days as a hero and bemoans a society that puts down people with extraordinary abilities. His wife, Helen, is happy putting their "super" past behind them, as she feels it jeopardizes their quiet, steady family life. Their son, Dash, is proud of his powers but doesn't feel they demand any respect or responsibility. His sister, Violet, fears her powers and can't control them as a result.

These different points of view provide *The Incredibles* with dramatic content until the main plot begins, when Bob is summoned to a mysterious island. These scenes of contention also offer a chance to explore the film's themes regarding mediocrity, uniqueness, and ability.

Characters as Plot Functions

Most of your characters will have a meaningful relationship with your protagonist. They will be their friends, lovers, mentors, or adversaries. However, some characters in your script will simply have a story function to perform. It's important to design these characters with care, so the mechanism that necessitated their existence isn't too transparent.

In *Brave*, Merida longs to have her destiny changed. This leads her to a witch. This witch doesn't have any meaningful opinions. She doesn't serve as a major obstacle in anyone's way, nor does she bond meaningfully with any other character. Her job—her function in the plot—is to grant Merida's wish and later issue the warning about the spell's irreversibility.

Despite this, Pixar created a character that seems to have her own life story. She tries to leave the witch business to become a wood carver, because of "too many unsatisfied customers." She sets off for a wood fair. Pixar even goes as far as to give her a strange affinity for bears. These small touches make her an interesting, funny, and unique character. It helps her stand out against the endless witches, warlocks, and Zoltans who have granted lost heroes their wishes since the dawn of storytelling.

Finding Nemo includes a virtual parade of characters who serve as obstacles in Dory and Marlin's quest. The vegetarian sharks are more interesting and original than a regular shark would have been. The surfer turtles essentially speed our heroes' journey to Sydney, but also impart some much-needed surfer wisdom.

It's good to keep in mind that there are no such things as small characters.

Pixar's devotion to ensuring that every character and detail in the worlds they create is original and entertaining is a great part of why their films are successful. All the inhabitants of Pixar's universes display some spark of creativity: from the small cleanup robot overly devoted to its job, to the sleazy manager of a travelling flea circus.

Keep Your Writing Honest

While it's important to create interesting characters with unique opinions and different attributes, you should never choose uniqueness or "coolness" over honesty. All your creations should have an emotional truth founded in reality. Dean Hardscrabble of *Monsters University* is terrifying in appearance and demeanor—but her approach is rooted in a very realistic and thought out pedagogical point of view. We've each probably had at least one teacher who shared Hardscrabble's beliefs.

The sequence in *Up* when Carl releases an endless cloud of balloons over his house and escapes the city is original, colorful, exciting, and moving. It also doesn't make any sense. Why would someone fly away in a house? Are there no planes to South America? Can't he just move somewhere else? It is a ludicrous action for a character to take. Which is why *Up* spends 20 minutes setting it up. We learn about Carl and Ellie's life together and the deep love they shared. How they dreamed about going together to Paradise Falls and how life kept forcing them to postpone their dreams—until it was too late. We also see Carl's current gray life and the chain of events that led to a court ruling ordering him to go to a nursing home while his house is set to be demolished by ruthless businessmen.

Under these circumstances, his actions make perfect sense. As a fugitive from the law, he uses his skills as a balloonist to escape without going through any authorities, while still hanging on to a meaningful part of his life with Ellie and setting off to fulfill their shared dream.

It's important to dream big and imagine outlandish events and characters. It is equally important to cement these moments in real, relatable emotions.

Designing Distinct Characters

Pixar excels at imagining a wide array of characters that are very different from one another. Of course, Pixar selects universes that offer ample opportunities for doing so: bugs, monsters, toys, superheroes, robots, fish, and cars come in all shapes and sizes. Their appearance influences their personality and behavior or is designed to suit them. The villainous Randal Boggs slithers around like a reptile. The likable Sully is essentially a big teddy bear with horns. The unintimidating physicality of Mike Wazowski is the basis for all of *Monsters*

University, which deals with his inability to scare. In *Toy Story 3*, Pixar gets a lot of mileage out of Slinky's and Mr. Potato Head's unique abilities (the tortilla sequence is a great example). You should likewise be sure to employ the possibilities that your character designs offer you.

The same is true when you're designing human characters. Consider the different princes who vie for Merida's affection. Their different physiques, manners of speech, and demeanors create the rich texture that makes *Brave*'s universe feel real.

Make your characters different emotionally and physically. Whether farmhands or finance brokers, actors or chefs, be sure to make each of your characters stand out.

Summary

Treat your story as an efficient machine. Every part of it should be treated with care and should be a part of your grand scheme. Nothing should be missing, and nothing should be redundant. This is especially true for your characters. While some characters may have specific functions to perform—obstacles, catalysts, and so on—they must also be drawn with care and imbued with their own stories and personalities. Never sacrifice honesty for originality or coolness. No matter what awesome invention you come up with, work hard to tie it to an emotional reality that is part of your fictional universe.

In *Inside Out*

Physically, the emotions in *Inside Out* are wonderfully designed. Each is distinctly different in a way that reflects their emotion: Anger literally fumes and blows his top; Joy is light and luminous. Because these characters are somewhat abstract—Joy, Sadness, Anger, etc.—the prism through which they see the world is very bold. If every character should have a clear point of view and a function, then pure emotions have all that built in. Each has their own set of concerns. For Fear, every day Riley doesn't die is a major success, while Anger wants everything to be fair.

Of course, these aren't the only inhabitants of Riley's mind. The many mind workers must exist both to populate the mind world and to advance or hinder our protagonists in their journey. Pixar mostly uses humor to disguise these characters' functions. Consider the guards of Riley's subconscious, arguing about their hats while a mad clown breaks loose; the Hollywood parody that consists of Riley's dreams; or the hard-boiled detective investigating a murder in Riley's imaginary Cloud City. These are bit parts, but they are created so that each offers the audience something—an insight, a laugh—rather than just moving the plot along.

Do It Yourself: *Review the characters and settings in your script. Are they all part of your core idea? Is there something missing? Is there something you can do without? Are any elements nothing more than perfunctory? What can you do to make your characters interesting, specific, or entertaining? Have you employed fun inventions retained only for their cool factor, but which are dishonest in their emotional truth? How can you fix that?*

CHAPTER 7

VILLAINS

"I am a nice shark,
not a mindless eating machine."
—Bruce

A Word about Antagonism

Antagonism refers to anything that stands between your
protagonist and their goal. It can be a character, an object, a
concept, or even the protagonist themself. In *Finding Nemo,* the
biggest antagonist is simply the ocean—its size, the creatures
it harbors, the ease with which one can get lost in it. Arguably,
distance is also an antagonistic force that Marlin must conquer.
Antagonists occasionally take the form of a truly nefarious
character—a villain, a Dr. Evil type—that cackles maniacally
as he watches the world burn. Often, though, they are a more
innocuous character who happens to inadvertently make life
harder for your protagonists.

This chapter focuses on sentient antagonists, as Pixar has crafted some very memorable ones.

Evil versus Troublesome

When discussing antagonistic characters, we must make a distinction between "evil" and "troublesome."

"Evil" characters have no regard for morals or fairness, and are indifferent or even joyous at the pain of others. Nevertheless, they should still have their own story and their own reasons for their actions. While Lotso's acts are inexcusable, his sad history makes him a rich, textured character whose actions, while villainous, are rooted in an emotional situation and behavior we can recognize and relate to. This makes his relationship with the toys more complicated and their struggle more meaningful than a simple "which side will win?" Everything that makes your protagonist interesting—an *existing flaw*, experience, point of view, idiosyncrasies—your villain should have too.

Villains make our protagonist's life harder because they enjoy malicious activities or because they prioritize their pleasure over someone else's wellbeing. Other antagonists may mean well but just happen to cause our protagonists grief. Let's call them "troublesome."

Up features both kinds of antagonists. Muntz is one of Pixar's clearer-cut villains. Yes, he has his reasons. He strives to restore his reputation by proving to the world that Kevin exists, but to do so, he is willing to not only capture and jail Kevin, but also to kill Carl and Russel. When someone is that indifferent to the harm he causes other people, we can easily put him in the "evil" category. However, *Up* has another big antagonist: Russel. Russel's innocence, determination, and Boy Scout values repeatedly derail Carl's attempts to disconnect from the living world and wallow in despair. This isn't Russel's intention. He isn't playing mind games with Carl or trying to wisely assist his personal growth. He's just in the right place at the right time. This concept connects to Pixar's use of a bonding plot, which often revolves around an antagonist that becomes an ally.

Pixar films often feature two main antagonists—one benevolent and one malicious—Buzz/Sid, Princess/Hopper, Jessie/Stinky Pete, Boo/Randall, and so on. *Ratatouille* has three main antagonists: One evil (Skinner), one benevolent (Linguini) and a third, Anton Ego. Ego isn't malicious the way Skinner and Muntz are, but I wouldn't call him benevolent either. He is the best kind of villain—a "good" one.

"Good" Villains

"Good" villains appear, on the surface, to belong to the malicious group. They are often mean, indifferent to the pain they cause, and even terrifying. What differentiates them from malicious antagonists such as Muntz or Hopper is that they have a benevolent core set of beliefs that strive to benefit their community. This is important. They can't be purely self-interested. Hopper's plans make life easier for the grasshoppers, but they ruthlessly damage the ants. The "good" villains—such as Anton Ego, Dean Hardscrabble, or the ship's autopilot in Wall-E—aren't nice, but they have positive core values. They never unfairly target anyone, and they don't enjoy hurting people. Their moral compass is in place, and they have certain lines they will never cross (unlike, say, Waternoose, who is willing to torture human children if it will solve Monstropolis's energy crisis).

Dean Hardscrabble and Anton Ego have been mentioned previously. Neither cares about the damage they leave in their wake. Ego was fine with Chef Gusteau's failure and death, which was a result of his review. Hardscrabble couldn't care less about the feelings of the students she heartlessly rejects.

Both are adamant about their beliefs.

As Ego explains, he doesn't just like food, he *loves* it. Ego believes it's his job to find great food and elevate it, while warning people about subpar meals. This is his quest in life. Yes, he is also extremely pompous and arrogant, which is why when Gusteau's becomes popular again, he is irked. It is a bad restaurant; how is it popular again? He must set this wrong right. But he isn't out to destroy Linguini and Remy the way Skinner is. Ego becomes their savior when they prove their worth to him and when they offer him a chance to make the world better (by promoting good food and culinary talent). Ego has integrity that goes beyond the self-serving actions of, say, Skinner.

Dean Hardscrabble is very similar. It is her job to locate those monsters that have the potential to become Scarers and then help them maximize that potential. Monsters that don't have what it takes—either because of a lack of skill or constitution—are a waste of her and the school's resources, thus harming the other Scarers and by proxy all of Monstropolis.

This brings us to the issue of proportionality. Had Dean Hardscrabble elected to enslave or kill those monsters that are slowing down the gifted monsters, she'd be back in malicious villain territory, and a fascist one at that. She chooses to just traumatically flunk those that are unfit. Thus, a "good" villain is one who acts only in service of their principles, and is not unnecessarily cruel in that pursuit.

You might argue that all villains have a value system that makes them believe their actions are right, and it's true. The difference is that usually these values are egotistical or perverted, and are rooted in hatred or joy at the pain of others. "Good" villains have some altruistic motive within them. They may stand in the way of your protagonists, but they have an important function in their community, which they perform with strict integrity.

Antagonists as Mirror Images

Some antagonists will have a thematic relationship to your protagonist. They will be a distorted mirror image, presenting our heroes with their darkest fears, or at least shining a light on their fallacies and weaknesses.

This is very apparent in *Toy Story 2* and *Toy Story 3*. Both Stinky Pete and Lotso are toys broken by the desertion of their owners. Both try to win over Woody and Buzz. They commiserate with them and offer them a seat at the table. At first, they seem to have a lot in common. It quickly becomes clear, though, that these antagonists represent what could happen to Woody and the toys if they don't resolve the *flaw* in their world. If Woody doesn't find a way to live without Andy, he will become like them: resentful and willing to do whatever it takes so that he won't ever be deserted again.

Other examples of this sort of connection can be found between Mr. Incredible/Syndrome, Gusteau/Ego, Wall-E/Auto, Carl/Muntz, and Merida/ Mordu.

Summary

A charismatic, cackling villain can be a lot of fun (especially when voiced by Kevin Spacey or Kelsey Grammer). Some of your stories will need those.

Keep in mind that many antagonists have good intentions and can be complex characters. When looking for antagonists to put in your hero's way, don't limit yourself to villains. Friends, supporting characters, and even the environment itself can provide you with plenty of dramatic fodder.

In *Inside Out*

Inside Out doesn't have a villain. The antagonistic forces in Joy's way are the terrain and inhabitants of Riley's mind—similar to Marlin's challenges in the vast ocean. Sadness is also a strong antagonist, of the troublesome kind. Her touch makes Riley sad, which is exactly what Joy is trying to avoid.

Lastly, Joy's own misconception of her role stands in the way of her goal. She thinks the best thing is for Riley to be constantly happy. This belief, in a way, is what propels the entire story to begin with. This is the existing flaw that needs fixing. Only when Joy realizes there's more to life than happiness does she accept the new system of complex emotions and allow Sadness to take her place in Riley's mind, which enables Riley to grow emotionally and overcome the crisis of moving to San Francisco.

Another set of conflicts exists on Riley's level of existence—her preoccupied parents, new school, the bubbling sadness within her. As mentioned, every emotional challenge Riley faces affects her and turns into a life-threatening disaster within the realm of her mind and vice versa.

Do It Yourself: *Who are the characters standing in your protagonist's way? Are they evil for the sake of evil, or do they have reasons for their maliciousness? How can you make them more understandable and relatable? Is there a way to make them benevolent while retaining the opposition they present to your hero? Are your characters' allies constantly helping them out, or do they challenge them as well? Friendship must be earned, and even then, it is there to challenge just as much as it is to support.*

CHAPTER 8

_____

DEVELOPING AN IDEA

*"The two of you did something together that
no one has ever done before. You surprised me."*
—Dean Hardscrabble

One of Pixar's greatest strengths is the studio's ability to surprise
us. We assume an aquatic adventure will feature sharks—but
vegetarian sharks? Many villains have dogs as sidekicks—but
rarely do they speak. And these are just flourishes. Pixar's
determination to avoid clichés pushes its stories and characters
to more interesting and exciting places than you'd expect. You
must carefully select which ideas you choose to develop into
full stories.

Equally important, if not more so, is how best to develop them.

Plotting versus Exploring

There are two main ways in which you can develop your idea. One is simply to explore your universe. If you're writing about a futuristic resort spaceship, wander around it with your mind's eye. What robots would it need? What utilities? What services would it offer? What would life be like on it? The spaceship in Wall-E is realistic because of the details Pixar came up with: the various robots that service the ship; the ways in which its denizens shop, eat, play, and socialize. They even created a very clear daily schedule for its captain. These details offer opportunities for set pieces, satire, and drama.

The other way to develop an idea focuses on the plan for your plot and characters. If you've decided that Marlin will find Nemo, you know the end of his destination. You must now design stops along the journey that will hinder and help him get there. These approaches aren't mutually exclusive. You'll often switch between them. One moment you are gathering information on your world and creating material for your story, and a moment later you are keeping or discarding your findings based on your plot's needs.

You don't have to keep every one of your discoveries, but you'll learn more about your fictional world. While it's important to stay focused on your core and theme, original ideas and creative sparks often come when you loosen the reins a bit. *Wall-E* is a prime example of this.

Wall-E uniquely combines two different but interconnected stories. One is the intimate, whimsical love story between Wall-E and Eve. The other is a battle of wills between a human captain and a spaceship's autopilot over the future of humanity. Regardless of which story came first while developing *Wall-E*, sticking too close to either story would have meant missing the other. Either way, it was Pixar's deep knowledge of this dystopian wasteland and their exploration of mankind's future history that gave them the material to intertwine these two stories.

Subvert Expectations

One of the great joys of Pixar's films is the way they subvert expectations. Whereas most superheroes use their powers freely to repeatedly save the day, in *The Incredibles* superheroes are forced to act "normal." Bob can't be Mr. Incredible by law. When developing your idea, discover what is expected from you, and then try to subvert those expectations.

A Bug's Life recalls the classic fable about the grasshoppers that starved in the winter after lazing about all summer. But in Pixar's version, rather than resign to starvation, the grasshoppers enslave the industrious ants.

These little twists are important, as they destroy familiarity and boredom. They keep the audience on their toes and surprise them at every turn.

Another mechanism Pixar excels at is adapting familiar settings into their fictional universe. Practically every frame of *Monsters University* offers a humorous twist on college life: fraternities, clubs, hazing, and traditions all remain socially and emotionally familiar, even as they are presented in the monster universe.

The end of *Toy Story 3* successfully and memorably subverts expectations set up by the two previous films. Andy has been an inseparable part of Woody's life. At the beginning of *Toy Story 3*, Andy is planning to take Woody with him to college. The film details the toys' imprisonment by Lotso. It depicts their escape, enacted just so they can all return to Andy and be part of his life—whether in the attic or in his dorm. However, at the end of the film, Woody decides it's time for him and Andy to part ways. For fans of the series, this is unexpected and would've been blasphemous had it not been handled with utmost honesty and emotion, creating a deeply moving conclusion.

Focus Your Canvas—Creative Limitations

As you develop your idea, it can be equally useful to decide which directions you will not pursue. By its genre and target audience, *Monsters, Inc.* was never going to feature its monsters destroying cities and eating children. Once this was decided, it forced the writers to think and decide what the relationship between these monsters and human children would be.

In his TED Talk, Andrew Stanton discusses some of the self-imposed limitations Pixar's writers decided on when they began, among them, not having a love story. Selecting that one limitation must've forced the writers to consider what the relationships in their films would then be, thus inevitably pushing them in new, interesting directions.

Brave features a princess, and princesses in films usually fall in love. However, Merida's suitors are tossed aside in favor of a story that deals with matters of responsibility, tradition, and maturity, while crafting a strong and interesting mother-daughter relationship.

Summary

Part of Pixar's success is due to the studio's originality and unique inventions. These stem from exploring your fictional universe and learning about all the places, people, emotions, and ways of life it has to offer. You don't have to use all your findings, but you should incorporate what helps you develop your plot and character arc. One of the best ways to explore your universe is to try to subvert expectations. Another way is to impose creative limitations on your story.

In *Inside Out*

Pixar did a lot of exploring of *Inside Out*'s unique setting. The structure of Riley's mind, as well as the many different mechanisms and creatures that inhabit it, can only be the result of an imagination allowed to roam. One can only imagine how many more jokes, characters, and places were discarded during development. Nevertheless, as imaginative as this world is, every part of it has a function. The subconscious serves as a prison. The huge chasm that is the Memory Dump, where thoughts are forgotten, offers death. The Islands of Personality are a strong visual metaphor for Riley's well-being. Every original part of the mind that the *Inside Out* writers chose to keep has a function in its plot.

The strongest instance of subverting expectations in *Inside Out* comes from the meaning it generates. We spend most of the film believing, as we often do in life, that sadness is a bad thing, a feeling to be quarantined or avoided. *Inside Out* wisely and maturely subverts this expectation and belief by allowing both Sadness and Joy to learn the role of sadness in Riley's emotional maturity.

Do It Yourself: *How much do you know about your fictional world? Have you allowed yourself to wander through its streets and fields, talking to its denizens, or did you only mine the parts needed for your plot? Consider the expectations from the material you're developing.*

Where can you subvert those expectations to create a moment that will surprise and delight your audience? If you're stuck, consider what you don't want to happen in your story world. Anything you eliminate will inevitably point toward something you would like to incorporate.

CHAPTER 9

_____

ENDINGS

"I hate it when someone gives away the ending."
—Hopper

Coincidence versus Character

Crafting a satisfying ending is one the biggest challenges you'll face as a writer. A good ending must make sense without being predictable. It should come with a bit of a surprise but also justify and elucidate the journey leading it up to it. One key way to reach this goal is to tie the ending deeply to the actions and constitution of your protagonist. The final action must be a direct result of the journey your characters have taken. In other words, avoid coincidences.

Coincidences happen in life. Random, statistically unfeasible things happen daily. But they can't happen to your characters, not when it counts. If you let your character's fate—good or bad—simply fall in their lap, you're robbing us of the joy of knowing who these characters really are. Think about the ending of *A Bug's Life*. A bird could've believably come down from the sky and eaten Hopper at any point in the film, but that doesn't make for a good story. When Flik knowingly lures Hopper near the real bird, however, risking his life by tricking Hopper into thinking that the bird isn't real, it becomes a personal victory. It becomes a chain of events that tells us something about bravery and about arrogance. Most important, we become involved in the action and experience the suspense. We witness the conflict, the two opposite forces, and wonder, "Who will win?" Will Flik manage to execute his plan and defeat Hopper, or will he fail? A random coincidence would rob the audience of that satisfaction.

Wall-E exhibits a degree of serendipity. Wall-E doesn't set out to save humanity, and, in fact, at no point is it implied that he even understands the changes he is effecting. However, he is *intentionally* trying to win Eve's heart, causing him to *intentionally* assist her in her directive, which is to keep the small plant safe. Everything that happens is a result of his attempts to fulfill this goal. Your protagonist may not quite understand or anticipate the effect of his journey, and that's fine, even desired. Could Marlin have predicted that trying to save his son would teach him to let his son enjoy more freedom? Could Sully and Mike have predicted that they would find an alternate, superior power source for Monstropolis? No. But they were all guided by clear goals and emotional compasses that led them to satisfying resolutions.

A coincidence occurs early in *Brave*. Merida visits a witch, asking for her mother to change. Of all the things in the world, the witch turns Merida's mother into a bear. Merida's father hates bears, ever since a particularly fierce one took his leg years ago. At first this seems like a contrived coincidence, designed to raise the stakes for Merida. However, as the story progresses we realize that another bear, Mordu, is a crucial part of the story. As the legend Merida's mother recited at the beginning of the movie comes true before our eyes, we realize that Elinor isn't the witch's first victim. Mordu is elevated from simply a threatening bear to a villain and more importantly to a poignant reminder of Merida's mother's fate if the spell isn't reversed in time. What begins as a coincidence turns out to be meticulously embedded into the story and values of the world, right down to suggesting the witch's obsession with bears. Mordu and Merida mirror each other. Mordu couldn't let go of his selfish desire to be stronger than ten men and control the kingdom. Merida, however, manages to change in time to bring her mother back by realizing her mother's importance in her life and her fate.

Back to the Beginning—Answering a Question the Audience Forgot

One way to craft a strong ending is to answer a question the audience has probably forgotten or hadn't even thought about but should have. Near the beginning of the third act of *Up*, Carl shakes off his bonds with Russel and Doug and sits inside his house in despair. In the safety of his house, Carl looks over Ellie's shared scrapbook, called *My Adventure Book*. He flips through old, beautiful memories, which are now marred by sadness and regret. We've seen this book before—we watched as the loving couple populated it with their experiences together. However, as Carl reaches the book's end, we discover that there was one page Carl (and the audience) didn't notice: a message from Ellie. She inscribed in the book: "Thank you for the adventure, now go have a new one." This message from his loved one encourages Carl to reconnect with Russel and Doug and go save Kevin.

This sort of pattern can be found in other movies: Mike making Boo laugh accidently early in *Monsters Inc.*, only to later use laughter as the solution to Monstropolis' power problems. Another example is Ego's closing monologue in *Ratatouille*, which is a reverse reflection of the words with which he opened the film.

Resolution–Showing the New, Healthy World

We've discussed how audiences love seeing characters change. This change, while satisfying, feels more meaningful and carries more weight when it creates a ripple effect. In many of Pixar's films, the journey the protagonists undertake often creates a better world for the people around them, fixing the flaw in the world.

This is most clear in *Wall-E, A Bug's Life,* and *Monsters, Inc.*
In all three films, the story that seems private at first carries
meaningful changes to the entire fictional world. Wall-E's quest
for Eve's love ends up bringing mankind back to Earth to grow
the first plant in hundreds of years. Flik's attempt to rectify the
damage and danger he brought on the colony ends up ridding
them of the threat of the grasshoppers forever and convincing
the colony to adopt his new, efficient methods. As mentioned
in the previous chapter, Mike and Sully's quest to bring Boo
back home ends up changing the very tenet upon which
Monstropolis relies: Instead of scaring children, you can get
more power from just making them laugh. Monsters don't have
to be monsters anymore.

These changes are often demonstrated visually. At the end of
Wall-E, we see the captain sowing the plant with a group of
kids. The ants in *A Bug's Life* are seen using Flik's machines
to harvest. *Monsters, Inc.* presents a particularly potent
visual. After an early shot showing all the monsters prepare
to scare— polishing their fangs, bloating themselves up,
extending their claws—we see them preparing to make the
children laugh (referencing famous comical gags) using similar
cinematic language.

The change doesn't always have to be on such a large scale.
It could be subtler. In *The Incredibles*, the family, as one unit,
cheers on Dash as he competes in running, using his power
without abusing it. In *Up*, Carl's inner change leads to Russel

having a father figure in his life, as witnessed by Carl attending his scout ceremony and giving him Ellie's Grape Soda pin, and later as they play together watching cars.

Summary

Your ending must be a reflection of your character and a direct result of the path upon which they were set. It shouldn't be expected or predictable, but it must be tied to your protagonist's journey. One way to create this effect is to have the ending relate to a seed you have subtly planted earlier in the film. Hopefully the audience forgets about that detail. When this seed pays off in your resolution, the audience will feel an increased sense of cohesiveness, strengthening the meaning of your ending. Pixar film endings often involve creating a better world. The most moving of endings show the positive results of the journey your character has taken, preferably in a visual way.

In *Inside Out*

The main forces that lead to *Inside Out*'s resolution are Bing Bong's self-sacrifice, Joy's tenacity, and her new understanding of Sadness's role in Headquarters. No coincidences there.

Joy's new understanding is prompted by one of those previously mentioned forgotten questions, in the scene when she reexamines Riley's hockey memory in the Memory Dump.

Earlier, she and Sadness had discussed a day in Riley's life. Sadness liked it because Riley missed a goal that cost the team the game. Joy liked it because Riley's parents and teammates all came to cheer her up. The audience notices these differing versions and registers the inherent conflict there, but forgets about it in favor of more pressing events: Riley running away from home, and Joy falling into the Memory Dump.

Stranded, Joy discovers the memory and rewinds it. She discovers that Sadness was indeed correct. Both versions were true. Furthermore, the sadness incurred by Sadness was what alerted Riley's parents and teammates, thus creating the happy memory Joy enjoys. For the first time, Joy grasps Sadness's purpose.

The resolution is visually presented through the color of the memories. At the beginning of the film, each memory had one tint, meaning it was colored by one emotion. By the film's end, however, Headquarters' shelves are filled with many dazzling multicolored memories. This is a great visual way to let us know that the emotions have learned to work together and as a result Riley achieves a richer, more complete and more mature emotional life. The new and more complex console, as well as the many new functioning Islands of Personality, are other visual cues that show Riley's growth.

Do It Yourself: *Is your ending a coincidence, or is it linked through a chain of causality to your character's actions? Does it tell us something new about your character's personality? Does your ending feel like an inseparable part of your story? Is it linked strongly to your plot through dramatic questions you've left unanswered until later in the story? Lastly, does your story create a ripple effect? Does it change something in the people, community, or world surrounding your protagonist? Is there a clear, potent visual way to express this change?*

CHAPTER 10

THEME

"Legends are lessons. They ring with truths."
—Elinor

What Is Theme?

Theme can be an elusive concept that can be approached in many different ways. For this chapter, let's treat theme as any abstract concept that your story is fundamentally about. What does your story present and explore that is universal and timeless? What is inherently human about it?

Finding Nemo is about a clownfish searching for his son amidst various oceanic dangers, but its theme is parenthood. *Ratatouille* is about a rat who wants to be a chef, but its main themes are creativity and individuality. The film also touches upon family, tradition, and criticism. *Cars* is about a race car longing to win an important race, but its theme is what we lose when we succumb to efficiency, modernity, and selfish goals.

Finding Nemo could change its entire plot and still retain its theme. It could be about an alien-being traveling the galaxy looking for its son (or daughter). Instead of sharks, you'd have Martians; instead of human divers, you'd have human astronauts. But if Marlin's motivations—as a grieving father obsessively committed to the safety of his son—remain unchanged, the film's theme would not change. Theme is what your story—your scenes, your chases, your one-liners—seeks to create and present.

Creating Theme, Step 1: Recognizing What Your Story Is About

Ideally, your theme arises organically from your story. *Toy Story* turned into a trilogy that unflinchingly depicts the relentless passage of time, the inevitable loss of childhood, and the irrelevancy that awaits us all—if we don't adapt and accept change and loss. All those things are inherent to toys. Pixar didn't necessarily set out to touch on these issues; the first film merely brushes against them. But once Pixar chose toys as their protagonists, these issues were bound to be introduced. Toys, as anyone who has ever revisited their childhood home can tell you, are doomed to be tucked away into boxes, closets, attics, and garages. For nostalgic reasons, putting away those toys is always sad and hard. Toys are also always in danger of being lost, forgotten, broken, or retired. Once Pixar chose toys as the film's protagonists, they had to address these themes. This exploration leads to the incredibly moving moments in *Toy Story 3.*

For other examples of Pixar themes, consider the world of ants that introduces issues of individuality (*A Bug's Life*), a family of superheroes that raises issues of fitting in and standing out (*The Incredibles*), a film about a college for monsters that explores mediocrity and dream fulfillment (*Monsters University*), and so on.

Creating Theme, Step 2: Permeate Your Theme Ubiquitously Throughout Your Story

Okay, let's say you've found your theme. It is an organic part of your universe, and even a part of your story. How can you make it clearer? How can you enrich it? How do you make it unique to your own fictional universe, rather than something trite? You must make your theme present in your universe. There are several ways to do so.

Ratatouille uses its supporting characters as paragons, as living manifestations of its theme. This is tricky to pull off. Sometimes such characters can come across as thin and one-dimensional or as mere proxies through which the author spouts personal beliefs. If you are creating a character as an embodiment of a value, it is often better to make it a supporting character. Create a complex environment that depicts struggles with different attitudes and values, and populate it with characters who embody aspects of your theme (which often are also the conflicting aspects of your main protagonist), as *Ratatouille* successfully does. Remy is torn: He is guided by Gusteau and threatened by Ego. These two represent the opposing edges on the spectrum of *Ratatouille's* theme.

The autopilot in *Wall-E* becomes a live embodiment of technology created by humans to make their lives easier, but which winds up making decisions for them and making them weak—a method the film uses to bring to life the historical process and thought processes that brought Earth to the state it is in when we are introduced to it.

To reinforce your theme, you can sometimes craft an antagonist as a reflection of your hero. Mr. Incredible thinks talent should be celebrated and people should be encouraged to stand out. Syndrome (his antagonist) wants to commoditize greatness, making sure that talent becomes irrelevant. Doc Hudson insists on keeping McQueen in town to make him pay for his rashness. McQueen is enamored with the racing world and blinded by his talent, thinking that winning is all that matters. Doc Hudson, as an antagonist, believes the opposite—and has the experience to prove it.

You can also imbue objects with thematic meanings. Consider the house in *Up*, for example. The prologue strongly sets up why Carl is so connected to the house and how much it represents his shared life with Ellie. The threat of parting with the house is what propels Carl to tie balloons to it and flee to South America. We quickly understand that the house is important to him— and why. Throughout the film, Carl literally carries the house around with him—just as he carries around the pain and grief of Ellie's death. Throughout the film, Carl jealously defends the house. But, slowly, the house deteriorates. The balloons tied to it pop. Its windows get broken. It becomes a little worse for wear. All this represents the still subconscious process of recovery that Carl goes through. At the film's climax, after Carl is encouraged by Ellie's words to start a new life, and after he decides to put himself in danger to save Kevin and Russel, he sacrifices the house to defeat Muntz. As the house slowly floats away from Carl, who knows he will never see it again, Russel offers his sympathy: "I'm sorry about your house." Carl replies: "It's just a house," thus signifying his inner change—his decision to move on and live despite his pain.

Brave also imbues its objects with further meaning to reinforce themes. In the universe of *Brave*, bears represent a dark side of humanity. They represent a wild, untamed embodiment of our dark, suppressed desires. Living in a bear's body is the punishment for those who can't find a healthy way of dealing with their repressed urges. In *Wall-E*, a short video from an old musical becomes the ultimate expression of love.

Most of Pixar's films simply assert their themes, or a variation on them, at some point or another. Dean Hardscrabble clearly states that her job is to "make great students greater, not make mediocre students less mediocre," thus emphasizing the film's theme of dealing with mediocrity.

Finding Nemo addresses its underlying debate about the dangers of overprotecting children when Marlin is in the belly of the whale (literally) and has lost all hope. He says, "I promised I'd never let anything happen to him." To which Dory wisely replies, "That's a funny thing to promise. You can't never let anything happen to him. Then nothing would ever happen to him."

In *Cars*, Doc Hudson flat out tells McQueen how selfish he is, pointing to his flaw and giving him a reason to change (the friends he made in Radiator Springs): "When was the last time you cared about something except yourself, hot rod? You name me one time, and I will take it all back. Uh-huh, didn't think so."

We have already discussed the thematic meaning of the opening and closing monologues in *Ratatouille*, as well as Gusteau's motto, "Anyone can cook!"

Summary

Theme is the part of your story that is universal and abstract. It isn't part of your plot. It is what your plot expresses. Your theme should emerge naturally from the fictional universe you've chosen to explore. Once you've found your theme, use plot, characters, locations, objects, and dialogue to make it as present as possible in your screenplay.

In *Inside Out*

Inside Out's climax is so thematically clear that it requires little elucidation: Feeling and accepting sadness (and fear, anger, and disgust) is important to our well-being. Emotions work best together, allowing us to feel the complex aggregate feelings within us, instead of trying to paint our life with one color emotion.

Inside Out uses images of multicolored memories as visual representations of its theme. These dazzling combinations of tints represent accepting the full richness of our emotions and the amazing inner world this acceptance cultivates. The dialogue also mirrors theme: Early on, Riley's mom commends her for remaining "our happy girl." However, in the film's climax, Riley says, "I know you want me to be happy, but…," admitting to her parents that she's sad, instead of trying to hold it in, in a futile effort to be happy.

Inside Out complements previous Pixar films and shows how the studio's selection of strong, universal, poignant themes is part of its strength.

Like *Finding Nemo* and *Brave*, *Inside Out* touches on parenthood and the dangers of parents forcing their expectations on their children. Like the *Toy Story* trilogy, Bing Bong's subplot deals with accepting irrelevance and the end of childhood, as well as the dangers of clinging onto something that is already gone. Childhood, family, sadness, maturity, death: These universal themes, placed at the core of our existence, are surprisingly underexplored in mainstream popular culture (compared with issues such as love or crime). Pixar's brave choice of themes and its equally brave (and wise) explorations of these themes are part of what sets the studio's films apart.

Do It Yourself: *What is your story about? What are the abstract questions or issues it flirts with or explores? Can you make these themes more present throughout your story via objects, dialogue, or characters?*

CHAPTER 11

THOUGHTS FOR THE ASPIRING ARTIST

"The world is often unkind to new talent,
new creations. The new needs friends."
—Anton Ego

This chapter is less about storytelling and more about your life as a creator. Pixar's films have offered us two texts that I believe are crucial to the education of any aspiring artist: *Ratatouille* and *Monsters University*. One deals with greatness, the other with the lack thereof. A smart, aspiring artist must consider that either possibility might end up relevant for them.

We discussed *Ratatouille* extensively in the first chapters of this book, so I will quickly recap. Remy is born with a gift. Pursuing his gift leads him on dangerous excursions but also brings him immense satisfaction. His rat community's reaction to his quest varies. His brother doesn't understand him but is supportive.

His father wants him to stick to the family business and not to leave him. But Remy does leave. And just as a theatre actor might end up in New York City, or as a screenwriter might end up in Los Angeles, Remy ends up in the best city imaginable for pursuing his talent: Paris. There he realizes he is at the very bottom of the food chain. No human will even let him be an assistant. No one believes that a rat like Remy could possibly have what it takes to be a great chef. He insists, supported by the words of his idol and mentor, Gusteau. He befriends some people. He gets his foot in the door of an upscale restaurant. This creates more dangers—sabotage by a jealous boss, and an attempt to co-opt his talent for creating mundane, boring products solely for monetary gain. Above everything else hovers the threat of ridicule. Will Anton Ego, the embodiment of all critics, of all criticism, approve of him? Will he like his work? Will he support it? Or will he knock Remy down like so many before him? Remy doesn't know what the outcome will be, but he tries. He picks a dish (the titular Ratatouille) and sends it out to Ego, eagerly awaiting his verdict.

Does that sound at all familiar? It should. Any aspiring artist probably relates deeply to Remy's situation. That's the power of theme. Remy didn't have to be a rat that wants to cook. He could have been a skunk that wants to make perfumes or a snake that wants to design sneakers (okay, clearly there's a reason I'm not writing for Pixar yet, but you get the point). The plot could change completely, but the theme would stay intact.

Even though none of us are rats, and most of us don't aspire to cook, we relate to *Ratatouille*'s theme.

Ratatouille encourages those of us who love cooking, writing, filmmaking, singing, programming, or anything else to pursue it. To not let any form of adversity—a push to conform, unsupportive peers, a closed industry, and of course, critics—hold us back.

Of course, *Ratatouille* has a happy ending. Ego not only approves of Remy but reevaluates his entire life philosophy. He says, "Not everyone can become a great artist, but a great artist can come from anywhere."

Remy clearly has a gift, but not everyone does. Even in the aforementioned speech, the film's victory lap, it is acknowledged that not anyone can become a great artist.

Monsters University focuses exactly on that kind of person. Mike Wazowski knew he wanted to be a Scarer ever since he was a kid. When he finally makes it to the best scaring program higher education has to offer, he has no doubt he will succeed. He studies harder than everyone. He helps other students. He knows everything there is to know about scaring.

And yet he is still kicked out of the program because, as the Dean puts it, he simply isn't scary. When a school competition offers him a chance back into the program, Mike whips a group of misfits into shape and brings them together to the finish line. However, he learns that no one, not even his friends, believes he is scary. Alone, and for the first time unsure of his calling, Mike puts himself to the ultimate test. He breaks school rules and risks his life to find the truth.

He tries to scare real human children and fails. Only then does he realize he isn't scary. After he and Sully are expelled, they find a want ad in the school newspaper for the mailroom at Monsters, Inc. They climb their way up the corporate ladder. Mike doesn't become scary, but he becomes a great coach—the best coach. We've watched him become a coach; it happened while he was trying to get back into the scare program. He'll never be a Scarer. He gave up on that dream. But he did find something he's good at, as well as friendship and satisfaction.

Yes, that could happen to you. You might discover that you're not meant to be a great cook, writer, filmmaker, singer, programmer, or anything else you're pursuing. And that's okay (which also happens to be the initials of Oozma Kappa, the fraternity Mike and Sully join—another subtle way of incorporating theme).

Monsters University tells us two things about giving up on our dreams.

The first is that we should only consider the possibility of giving up after we've tried our very best in every manner we can imagine. Mike doesn't quit when Dean Hardscrabble kicks him out. He doesn't quit when all his friends fail him. He quits only when he is faced with objective, irrefutable evidence that he isn't scary, when he has no other option other than to accept who he is.

The other thing *Monsters University* tells us is that Mike's pursuit of his dream was not in vain. Not only because he made friends, but because the pursuit did lead him to his calling—it just wasn't what he thought. Mike ends up being the coach of the best Scarer in Monstropolis. And anyone who watches *Monsters University* can't deny that Mike is a great coach. And he never would have discovered his coaching talent if he hadn't pursued his dream.

These ideas are deeply embedded into the stories of *Ratatouille* and *Monsters University*. From setting to character to dialogue to plotting, the films are constructed in ways that explore these themes and express opinions on them. (And, of course, they entertain!) Apart from the immense craftsmanship, creativity, and heart, you can also learn from these films' core themes: Don't let anyone stop you from pursuing your dream, and don't let pursuing your dream stop you from finding something that you're good at and that makes you happy.

ACKNOWLEDGMENTS

This book would never have been finished without the help of several people. My deep thanks to Gleni Bartels, for her copyediting work; Stuart Weinstock, for his helpful observations; Ayelet Dahan, for her sharp eye and insightful suggestions; Dan Foster, for his thoughtful and meticulous editing and proofreading; Danielle Foster, for the book's composition; and, of course, Morr Meroz, for his endless support and for giving this book a wonderful home under the auspices of Bloop Animation.

This book wouldn't be complete without humbly thanking Pixar's great storytellers, who have given us so much joy, laughter, sadness, insight, and inspiration throughout the years.

Most importantly, thank you, dear reader, for making it all the way through. I hope you found the ideas presented here useful—and that if you didn't, at least they serve as a stone on which to sharpen your own thoughts on storytelling. Either way, I hope the experience propelled you to write more—stories, scripts, shorts, plays, books, poems, tweets—anything. Keep on writing until your output catches up with your standards. And, oh, what a glorious day that will be.

FILMOGRAPHY

Toy Story (1995)

Directed by John Lasseter

Original Story by John Lasseter, Pete Docter, Andrew Stanton, and Joe Ranft

Screenplay by Joss Whedon, Andrew Stanton, Joel Cohen, and Alec Sokolow

A Bug's Life (1998)

Directed by John Lasseter, Co-Directed by Andrew Stanton

Original Story by John Lasseter, Andrew Stanton, and Joe Ranft

Screenplay by Andrew Stanton, Donald McEnery, and Bob Shaw

Toy Story 2 (1999)

Directed by John Lasseter, Co-Directed by Lee Unkrich, Ash Brannon

Original Story by John Lasseter, Pete Docter, Ash Brannon, Andrew Stanton

Screenplay by Andrew Stanton, Rita Hsiao, Doug Chamberlin and Chris Webb

Monsters Inc. (2001)

Directed by Pete Docter, Co-Directed by Lee Unkrich, David Silverman

Original Story by Pete Docter, Jill Culton, Jeff Pidgeon, Ralph Eggleston

Screenplay by Andrew Stanton and Daniel Gerson

Finding Nemo (2003)

Directed by Andrew Stanton, Co-Directed by Lee Unkrich

Original Story by Andrew Stanton

Screenplay by Andrew Stanton, Bob Peterson and David Reynolds

The Incredibles (2004)

Written and Directed by Brad Bird

Cars (2006)

Directed by John Lasseter, Co-Directed by Joe Ranft

Original Story by John Lasseter, Joe Ranft, and Jorgen Klubien

Screenplay by Dan Fogelman, John Lasseter, Joe Ranft, Kiel Murray & Phil Lorin, and Jorgen Klubien

Ratatouille (2007)

Directed by Brad Bird, Co-Directed by Jan Pinkava

Original Story by Jan Pinkava, Jim Capobianco, and Brad Bird

Screenplay by Brad Bird

Wall-E (2008)

Directed by Andrew Stanton

Original Story by Andrew Stanton and Pete Docter

Screenplay by Andrew Stanton and Jim Reardon

Up (2009)

Directed by Pete Docter, Co-Directed by Bob Peterson

Story by Pete Docter, Bob Peterson, and Tom McCarthy

Screenplay by Bob Peterson and Pete Docter

Toy Story 3 (2010)

Directed by Lee Unkrich

Story by John Lasseter, Andrew Stanton, and Lee Unkrich

Screenplay by Michael Arndt

Brave (2012)

Directed by Mark Andrews and Brenda Chapman, Co-Directed by Steve Purcell

Story by Brenda Chapman

Screenplay by Mark Andrews, Steve Purcell, Brenda Chapman, and Irene Mecchi

Monsters University (2013)

Directed by Dan Scanlon

Story by Dan Scanlon, Daniel Gerson & Robert L. Baird

Screenplay by Daniel Gerson & Robert L. Baird, and Dan Scanlon

Inside Out (2015)

Directed by Pete Docter, Co-Directed by Ronnie del Carmen

Story by Pete Docter and Ronnie del Carmen

Screenplay by Pete Docter, Meg LeFauve, and Josh Cooley

BIBLIOGRAPHY

Campbell, Joseph. *The Hero with a Thousand Faces*. New World Library; Third edition (July 28, 2008)

Vogler, Christopher. *The Writers Journey: Mythic Structure for Writers*. Michael Wiese Productions; 3rd edition (November 1, 2007)

Stanton, Andrew. "Andrew Stanton: The Clues to a Great Story." TED. February 2012. https://www.ted.com/talks /andrew_stanton_the_clues_to_a_great_story?language=en

Made in the USA
Las Vegas, NV
16 February 2024

85890672R00070